BORN PARANORMAL

A LIAR'S STORY

DAVID C. KIEFER

FIRST PRINTING EDITION MMXX

Copyright © 2020 David C. Kiefer

Contents

Forward

Call me a liar! Do it now! And don't worry, I'm used to it. Now that we've gotten that out of the way, I'd like to tell you a story. Up until now, I have never disclosed this story, or the myriad of experiences that make up my life, with more than a handful of people. Everyone has little bits of my story, including my family, but no one has all of the details.

Even as I write these words, I'm struggling with coming to grips with my past—and how those events shaped the man I am today. In fact, you may consider this book my introduction to the world as well as an attempt to rationalize what most normal people would call para- or ab-normal.

This line of thinking brings me to the following question. What is normal? We use the term all of the time. We think we understand what it means. But I'm not so sure. What does normal actually mean?

I have often found myself pondering what that word means, and as we proceed throughout the following pages, you will no doubt understand why.

There have been countless conversations, articles, and whole books dedicated to the concept of normal, what it means, how we determine it, what the implications are, who is and isn't normal, and those sort of things. I'd even go so far as to say that most people spend at least some portion of their lives wondering if they are normal in the proverbial quest to fit in.

So, here are the stats. The National Institute of Mental Health (NIMH) estimates that over 25% of Americans have some form of mental disorder. Someone with a mental disorder has behaviors, feelings, and thoughts that deviate from what broader society defines normal. These norms vary from culture to culture (i.e., what's normal or typical in one culture may be completely atypical in another culture).

If you're living just beyond the boundaries of what your society determines as normal, you may have some lingering negative side effects. At least, that was true for me, which is why I've always been so intrigued with the topic.

All throughout my life, especially the younger years, I pondered what normal meant, typically in the sense of trying to figure out whether or not my circumstances aligned with the majority of other people's experiences. In hindsight, it would seem that what I experienced–and what I try to describe in the following pages–is anything but normal.

I'm reminded of something Albert Einstein once said.

"A human being is a part of the whole called by us 'universe', a part limited in time and space. He experiences himself, his thoughts and feeling, as something separated from the rest, a kind of optical delusion of his consciousness. This delusion is a kind of prison for us, restricting us to our personal desires and to affection for a few persons nearest to us. Our task must be to free ourselves from this prison by widening our circle of compassion to embrace all living creatures and the whole of nature in its beauty," according to Einstein.

He was telling us that even though we experience the world as being disconnected from the rest, it's not true; in fact, he calls this sense of disconnectedness a delusion. The truth is we are all connected on a much deeper level than we will ever fully understand.

Therefore, what some people call para (or out of) the norm isn't really all that para-normal after all.

At the same time, when evaluating ourselves, we tend to decide how to act based upon prior perceptions of what we deem normal. If we take it one step further, normal also means average or standard. However, for me, it's always been much harder evaluating my own behavior, which complicates matters even further.

I admittedly have no clue what is or should be considered "normal."

That framing just doesn't occur to me like it does most people. My friends and family can attest to that, and if I were being honest, I am a bit of an oddball. Call it my charm or wit or way of looking at the world. None of it is "normal."

Moreover, this fleeting, subjective notion of normal relates to the concept of "real," as well. "Real" is a bit of a pet peeve of mine. I cannot stand it – just like the word normal. The term real is an adjective that tends to correspond to nouns such as man, woman, or food. For example, we might say, "Now, that's a *real* man." Or, we might say, "That's some *real* food." But what does real even mean? If that's a *real* man than who is everyone else? Am I not real? I may not be "normal," but am I real?

I am real, but I may not be what other people consider "normal," and that's alright by me. Of course, it hasn't always been that way.

I came to realize that normal is completely made-up and an often altogether false construct. It is an arbitrary notion and has no real meaning beyond what we as a society or you as an individual apply to it. There is no normal. Normal for me is not the same as normal for you, and I have come to accept that. Can we admit it here and now for the record that those things are indeed true?

We look at the external world and everything in it and we try to make sense out of things. We struggle seeing our role in the greater universe. We cannot sense the connectedness that ties us all together. And what normally happens is that we try to fit everything into neat, little boxes, so that we can understand the world around us better.

And when it doesn't fit in that box? We cast it aside as unbelievable, unreal, or dare I say, a lie.

I guess that makes sense. But what's not understandable is drawing these hard lines in the sand and saying that everything that is normal is acceptable and everything that falls outside the bounds of normality is unacceptable. Afterall, I agree that your normal is not the same as my normal. That's certainly true of my life, as you will come to see.

My normal was everything but normal. In fact, by most standards, my normal isn't normal even to this day. What is normal are the commonalities that we find, all those similar-but-a-little-bit-different experiences that bind us together.

As Einstein pointed out, we each experience life differently from our hopes, our thoughts, our dreams, and our actions. We experience the world in a way that is completely unique to us, but that's what makes us all human. In fact, that's part of the beauty of this world.

I may be an intrepid adventurer, but I happen to think that life would be very bland if everyone and everything looked, tasted, felt, and acted the same.

Life is about all of the intimate, first-hand experiences that make each one of us unique and special. The only normalcy, therefore, is what we experience first-hand with our own senses. That's what normal means to me.

I can tell you all about what that normal looked like and how it evolved over time. Those are the unique details of my story that make me who I am. The fact that many people found these things to be unbelievable or disagreed with them is irrelevant. Some people are just closeminded and hard to reach.

But that's not always the case.

We have made tremendous advancements in the industry and acceptance of the paranormal is at an all-time high and I felt like it was time to finally tell my story.

I told bits and pieces of my story for years, but I stopped telling it because of a general lack of acceptance. For years, decades even, I sat silent on my story , rarely telling it. Meanwhile, my family didn't discuss it amongst themselves (not one peep even though we and everyone close to us knew it to be true).

With the wider spread acceptance of these type of events today, I think it's time. It's time to shake the cobwebs in my mind loose and tell all the stories once again and with greater detail and precision than ever. It's time to let the world know what normal looked like for my family and I.

Perhaps my normal will be similar to yours! If that's true, will we redefine normal together? Let's wait and see...

CHAPTER 1
A Great Family Divide

I grew up in St. Louis, Missouri. I was born to two doting parents, and I had five siblings. The oldest, Paul Henry, died at childbirth. Although I never met him, I always try and remember him for who he was and could have been.

Paul Douglas was 13 and already 6 feet tall. He was thin and didn't have much muscle but was tough. To me, he had no fear. He was Dad's dutiful second in charge, sometimes even before Mom. If Dad wanted us kids to get something done, he gave it to Paul, who was kind and highly intelligent.

Like Dad, he read anything he could get his hands on. And he was equally athletic. After the move, he joined several athletic teams at school, as well as the debate and drama clubs. Paul also possessed traits of my grandfather (on Mom's side).

He was kind, gentle, and patient, and he rarely lost his cool. If anyone was a blend of Mom and Dad, it was Paul! I mean, he just always seemed to do the right thing, or at least it appeared that way. He seemed to always have a moral compass that steered him in the right direction. It was as if he was born with it in him.

When we were young, Paul would often play hero to Matt- the youngest, defending him from any issues I had with him, sometimes physically. Because of this, Paul and I had a strained relationship for a long time. Part of it was because I saw him as an authority (which I will explain more later). And part of it was because he was Matt's defender.

But it was also because of the ten year age gap between us, which seemed more significant back then. I am sure, for him, I was just another kid to keep in line for Mom and Dad. But as adults, we became quite close. In fact, he used to introduce me as "My best friend happens to be my brother." Now, that always made me proud.

Mary was 9 and was just as patient as Paul at that age. Although she was still young when we moved, she was very popular at school. She had a way of talking to anyone and was very kind. Shortly after moving, she received honors for her grades. Around the house, she was Mom's right hand.

She would sometimes get stuck with the tasks of cleaning the house or taking care of us kids. And, at the beginning, she did it without hesitation. We still joke about how much I made her make Tang for me. But as much as she was Mom's right hand, she was a daddy's girl, too.

Mary loved Dad, and it was obvious. For dad, Mary would do anything to see the pride in his eyes. Mary and I have been close all our lives. Maybe it was our common continual love for Dad or something else. I'm not sure.

At age 8, Susan was a challenge, especially for me. She often treated me mean and would say nasty things. I could not understand it at the time. *What did I do to her?* I wondered. It was not until we got older and discussed it that she admitted she harbored some jealousy over me when I came into the picture and took the youngest spot title from her.

So, I would come to understand how she felt later when Matt did the same thing to me, and I felt a strong sense of jealousy up close and personal. Susan was just as smart as Paul and Mary. She received honors in school and was very popular, too. Unlike Mary, though, she excelled at sports. Volleyball was her favorite. She had a commitment to it like nothing else. Like my relationship with Paul, it wasn't until we got older that Sue and I had a good relationship, one we didn't have as children.

It wasn't until a year after we moved that Matt came along. I was always jealous of Matt as a kid. He got Mom and Dad's attention purely out of need. Because of this, he also got to go to town, go to stores, and got more alone time with them. Matt was naturally a loner. He wanted to play, but only when he wanted to do so. Later in life, like my other siblings, Matt and I became very close, and I learned of his struggles at that time and later. To this day, we are still close. But for now, he was just "the baby" taking Mom and Dad's attention from me.

With four – soon to be five of us- under one roof the house was always a buzz with activity. I cannot grasp what my parents had to deal with having all of us and having to raise us.

Mom's family was strict Roman Catholic Italians. They were a tight-knit group. We were surrounded with grandparents, aunts, uncles, great aunts, cousins, and extended family, all of whom loved us and each other dearly.

Every Sunday, we had big family dinners that filled the table with home-cooked meals with recipes from the Old Country. We were from "The Hill" in St. Louis. For those of you who may be unaware, "The Hill" is a neighborhood where Italians live. Think Little Italy or something along those lines.

They had been in that area since before 1954. Back then, the church, Saint Ambrose, was the rock of the neighborhood. Hundreds of good Italian families sent their kids there to learn. Both my mom and my aunt went to Saint Ambrose, as well. Both of them graduated the Catholic high school, so it must have been a huge surprise when my mom decided she was going to break from the tradition and join another church.

My father's family was different. My father was raised by his step Dad. He was a gruff man who looked like a bulldog to us younger kids. Grandpa instilled fear in us, and, as I got older, I came to realize his gruff exterior was the results of everything he'd been through as a child.

As family legend goes, my grandparents met when my grandmother was only 15. My father's Dad died during World War II shortly after my grandmother became pregnant. His family disowned her and even blamed her for him leaving for war if you can believe that. So, my grandmother raised my father on her own until she remarried.

Shortly after, Uncle Bill came along. He seemed to always have his you-know-what together from the way he dressed to the way he talked to his whole persona. He even played professional ball for a while, lived out of state, and was always moving on to bigger and better things throughout his life. He didn't come through often. But when he did, his visits were a big to-do, and we were very excited to hear all of his stories!

Family gatherings with my father's side of the family were exceedingly rare. When they did occur, it was usually my grandmother cooking a big meal followed by the adults watching one of those evangelical preachers on television. They'd sit there talking back to the TV as if he could talk back to them.

Grandmother was a bit of an odd bird. I realized even back then as a child that she was just different. She had lived a hard life. She had no fear of telling anyone about her hard life. Later we would learn there were some convenient inaccuracies in all of her stories. At the same time, I'm sure her life really was hard even if her stories didn't always add up. For example, she always maintained she was raised in the woods of Arkansas. She said her father preferred it that way. She would talk about her stepmother who was 100% Native American, saying how mean she was and how she would whip her for the slightest reason she could find.

She would recall being dirty all the time and unable to keep herself clean. She said when more and more people started moving to the area it became too much for her father to deal with. So, the whole family—uncles, aunts, cousins—packed up and moved to the middle of Tennessee. I'm even told the small family place evolved into a small Tennessee town, which still exists to this day. I still have relatives there but have never met them or been there to see for myself.

Grandmother would beam with pride when she talked about her family life, growing up.

"Our family still lives in the holler named after our family," she explained with pride.

As she tells it, she later became a police officer in St. Louis County after moving to the area. At that time, women were still not allowed on the street, so she took a position as a dispatcher. She told us it was one of the hardest jobs she ever had.

She recalled, "You would think it was easy because you were sitting at a desk and not out on the street, but your stomach acid could burn a hole straight through you on some days waiting for a response to know if the officer on the other side was okay. Your heart would hang moment-to-moment waiting on confirmation that would sometimes never come."

She later worked for an alcohol licensing bureau. Her time in law enforcement and government ultimately hardened her into the tough, no sass grandmother we all knew and loved.

My parents were different. I don't just mean different from their parents, although they indeed were. I mean, they were different from each other, representing extreme opposite ends of the spectrum. In fact, I often wonder how the two of them ever got together and tolerated each other long enough to have five kids. Excuse me, six kids. (I try to never forget about little Paul Henry, rest his soul.)

The thing about my mother that stands out the most to me was that she was always all about two things, the church, and God. I believe Mom found something in church that moved her, and that same something just never moved Dad. It was as if she had a need to be there and was attracted to the church like a magnet.

Now, in hindsight, maybe it was the social aspect of it that kept her coming. Or, maybe it was more religious (or both). I cannot say for sure. But, at least for me, there always appeared to be a faux side to her drive to be religious. Outwardly, she would recite scripture, attend church every time the doors were open, and socialize with others from the church. So, church was a big part of her life; and because it was a big part of her life, it would always have some effect on my own life.

To be honest, there was always something that left me questioning her motives. Don't get me wrong, technically she did everything right, but her heart never seemed to be into what she was doing. It was like she was just going through the motions.

There was a whole fake façade to my mother's religious beliefs or the way she applied and followed those beliefs. For example, we never had Christmas. We could have presents on our "fake Christmas," but only if we didn't call them Christmas presents.

Technicalities around birthdays were even more complicated. We could receive a card on or around our birthday, but it could be a "birthday card," even though it could (and would) say that. Accordingly, any gift was not a "birthday gift." It was a gift someone happened to choose to give you at the exact same time as your birthday because they happened to see you and wanted to give you something.

We could gather with family and have whole dinners that happened to correspond to various holidays, but we could never call it a _____ [insert the name of any holiday] meal.

There were so many contradictions.

If by chance toward the end of November we decided to sit down and have a large family meal with relatives from near and far and decided to give thanks for what we appreciated over the past year, and if that meal happened to include ham or even turkey and be on the exact day everyone called "Thanksgiving," that was fine. We could do that. But it was not a "Thanksgiving dinner" because we could not acknowledge that particular holiday as being Thanksgiving.

If you're scratching your head or even laughing out loud at this point, don't be ashamed. I often found myself laughing too. A lot of us laughed. I wondered whether or not a "god" or higher power who created all things couldn't easily see through the charade. I wondered, as a child, if I could get away with the same things that religion was passing off as good reasons to do certain things.

"No, Mom. I didn't go to that party. I happened to be in a place where other people were gathered with alcohol, loud music, and dancing. They chose to gather and do certain things by pure happenchance. It was going on all around me. Although there was alcohol present, I did not call it a party, so therefore, it was not a party," I might assure her.

It wouldn't fly, though. Not even today.

These were some of the technicalities and loopholes we had to navigate because she wanted to shoehorn religion into a neat box, and have it work how she needed it to work for her.

It was extremely exhausting.

It's like intellectual spaghetti. The contradictions, the seemingly illogical positions asserted. It was all too much to bear, even at a young age. I knew it wasn't right. And it turned me and everyone else off. So, it had the opposite effect she was probably going for.

Mom's drive-by religion meant church every Sunday morning and night and Wednesday evening as well as Bible study once or twice per week. Add in other services or activities throughout the week, and it kept us all very busy. Perhaps that was the point.

We were not allowed to associate with people who were not the same religion as us either. At least, not at first.

I was reciting scripture long before I started school. My siblings and I dared not to say we had free time or act bored. If we did, we were told to sit nearby and read our Bibles so loud she could hear us. There was no way to fake our way through the reading.

Mother was short and reasonably slim but not at all petite. She reminded me of this little super religious worker bee who was a constant buzz of activity and never ceased. There were five of us kids. She was always doing something, even more so when Dad was around. She could keep up with him and afterward wrangle us to get dinner onto the table.

Dad was her polar opposite when it came to religion and just about everything else. Mom was short. Dad was tall. His stature commanded attention, eclipsing 6'7" with size 14 shoes. Yet, he was reserved. He rarely raised his voice, at least while I was younger. He didn't have to. When Dad spoke people listened. He would also read all the time. There was a calmness to him that almost offset Mom's activity. His words were well thought out. Precise.

Not Mom.

She always had something to say, a question to ask, an opinion to give, a story to tell. She was apparently so bad as a child about talking all the time that my grandfather would joke, she must have been vaccinated by a Victrola (record player) needle.

Unlike Mother, Father wasn't religious. I mean, he read the Bible numerous times. He knew it backward and forward from memory and could hold an intelligent discussion about it with anyone. But his spiritual interests took him much further than that. He had some Native American beliefs and was very spiritual.

Though my grandmother would talk about her stepmother harshly, for example, my father would talk about her lovingly. He often said when he was barely able to walk his grandmother started taking him through the woods on "Papa's land" and told him the purpose of every single plant they encountered. She made a game out of it. She would pick a plant, and he would spout its name, and it's multiple uses.

As he got older, he retained the knowledge and would spout the names and uses of a range of plants.

"Did you know the Native Americans never used or created the word weed?" he asked. "They didn't know what a weed was. It was a white man's construct and came along much later. They knew every plant and every plant had a distinct purpose."

Father was a very wise man.

We spent countless nights listening to him tell stories or spout facts about Native Americans. He would tell engaging tales about the great American Indian tribes, their history, and habits. He would dream of living off of the land and "being free."

He was tied to nature and the land. It was a part of him, like breathing is a part of you or me.

I cherish those stories and would give anything to flashback in time and hear just one more.

While he was close to nature, he was also militant in his beliefs. We didn't know why back then, but we came to understand later. Dad had a way of seeing family (and really just about everything) tactically. He would explain how if we functioned as a battalion there was nothing we couldn't do.

He would hold out his giant, meaty paw up in the air and proclaim, "The five of you are like five separate fingers on my hand. One finger can do a few things on its own. With two fingers, you can do a little bit more. Add three, four, or five fingers, and you can do a lot more than that," he said moving his fingers back and forth as he spoke.

"When times get tough or you have a need, you can work together like a battalion and get through anything. Think of it like a closed fist that's solid enough to punch right through anything," he continued. "Now, that's what family is all about. Each one of you 5 kids represents one finger on this hand," he added, pointing with his free hand to his fist.

I looked up at him with amazement as he waved his fist high in the air. His eyes were beaming with pride as he taught us the lesson.

You see, in his eyes, the family unit is uniquely designed to function like a team. Each part of that team has the distinct purpose of supporting everyone else and making the whole unit stronger. Of course, that meant if there was a weak link somewhere, it was a problem for everyone. Failure to do your duties meant failing the whole team, and that was very bad because you weren't just letting yourself down. You were letting everyone else down.

That's how Dad talked.

My older siblings talk about Mom and Dad and all of the loving memories they had of them. But by the time I came along, things were much different.

I had a first-hand account of the struggle between Mom and Dad. First, as a child, then as a young man, and beyond. There was a great schism between the two concerning their beliefs, and it would prove impossible to bridge.

How they got together in the first place, no one probably understands but them (I doubt they do either). How they eventually married and had five (six) kids is even more of a mystery.

Their relationship defies logic even as I reflect back on their lives, the different beliefs, and the unusual dynamics between the pair.

They were in a constant state of tug-of-war between one another reflective on the surface—and lurking just beneath the surface like a massive iceberg. In other words, much of the struggle could not be seen—but it could certainly be felt.

When Dad would tell us stories, Mom would leave the room. Sometimes she would cut him off entirely. She just couldn't stand to hear him talk about his experiences and beliefs. At other times, when she would press for Christianity or push hard to get us to read the Bible (or certain church teachings), Dad would make sure to be gone. The way she couldn't stand his beliefs, he felt equally as impassioned against hers, as well.

As you can imagine, Dad never attended church, Bible study, or any Christian event with us; yet, to this day, he is the most spiritual person I have ever met in my life. Does that make sense? He was wiser than we knew or came to understand. It would take decades for us to piece things together and make sense out of the life—and career—of my father.

. . .

AT THE AGE of three, we moved south of St. Louis to a small town in rural Missouri. It was a small, picturesque midwestern town where everyone knew each other (or knew someone who did).

There was one grocery store, one fast food restaurant, and one traffic light in the entire town. On weekends, main street was packed with people cruising up the small strip.

Picture this: cars would drive back and forth over and over for hours. You'd see some barely pubescent teenage boy hanging out of the passenger side window of his best friend's car waiving at girls as they drove by. People were laughing and cutting up and blowing their horns. There was a designated spot on each end of the strip where people would turn and then head back the other direction, and they would do this repeatedly for hours.

It's hard to imagine now, but that was considered fun back then. It's not like we had a lot of places to go or things to get into. However, our small town did have one of the churches.

Dad worked in the city and would come home on the weekends. Mom kept us focused on school, and the new church she had discovered, making that easier.

We lived on a modest four-acre lot that provided us with a place for our imaginations to wander. There was a large field nearby, some woods, and a pond.

The house was great. There was plenty of room for us to explore. But even as a kid, the house seemed just a little bit weird. I know it was the 1970's with bright greens and oranges being the prevailing colors of choice. But our house was different.

My friend's homes had bright colors and felt warm and inviting. Whereas our home was dark with black faux counters, black vinyl floors, blood-red carpet, and dark brown (almost black) kitchen cabinets.

There was the basement, which was mostly unfinished but for some unpainted drywall, and it was divided into two large sections.

Then there was the fireplace.

When I say fireplace, I'm not speaking about one of those small ones you see nowadays.

This fireplace was odd, and it seemed like it was out of place, like it had been transported from someplace else and dropped onto the basement. It took about half of the width of the entire house from concrete to beam, floor to ceiling. It was semi-circular in the front with a ledge that ran down the full width of the fireplace, bringing it to eye level. It was huge! Oh, and did I mention it was built out of the blackest lava rock on planet earth? This was not a fireplace. It was a monument, an altar, and a statement. And as a child, it sent my senses tingling.

There were some of the more popular lighter colors throughout the house, but very few. The house seemed darker than any other house I have ever been to. It's almost like the house would suck all the light out of the air like a black hole. Yeah, it was weird, but it was our home.

Dad still worked in the city, so weekends meant Dad was home from work, and we were directed to be on our best behavior. Each child had assigned duties, even at the tender age of two and three.

Things were made abundantly clear. Should Dad come home and find out we did not do what we should have done while he was gone there would be a steep price to pay. Of course, as a young kid the rules were more relaxed for me for a time, but, even still, they were there, and we all knew what they were.

Dad would arrive late on Friday nights, usually after we had all went to bed. We would wake up on Saturday mornings and find him either waking us up for chores or already at the kitchen table having breakfast with Mom. Breakfast conversations were light and focused primarily on school or the previous week's goings ons.

Dad had a most unusual job but never discussed anything about his work, and we knew not to ask. He would steer the conversation toward how we were doing at school. He would tell us he worked to be with his family, not the other way around. That was that.

After breakfast and a briefing from Mom about the week's events, there was "accountability" where he would hear our confessions about any failures to do with our chores or school. If there were no failures, things were great. If one of us failed to do something the past week, there was a discussion followed by a spanking followed by extra chores for the following week for that kid. Then, it was off to spend the rest of the time helping with chores around the house, working in the garden, splitting and chopping wood, cutting grass, or any other chores dad saw fit.

After dinner, we entertained each other by putting on a play for our parents, doing puzzles, playing board games, listening to one of Dad's stories, or having him play piano, while we sang along. He was an exceptional musician.

Television in our household did not come around until much later. It was never a big part of our lives. Everyone else in the neighborhood had the fancy color televisions. Not us. When we did get one, it was an old black and white early model, a cheap leftover from the 1950's Grandma and Grandpa dropped off after they upgraded.

On Sundays, it was church followed by dinner. Then Dad packed up and headed back to the city for work. For us, it meant what little bit of excitement we had was gone for now, and the routine of school, church, and chores settled back in quickly. We had very limited time to actually play in the field or woods and stare at clouds in between our activities.

This was my normal for a spell. Yes, my younger brother came along about a year later to grow the clan to five- no six (Paul Henry). But things really didn't change all that much. Afterall, to me, Matt was only a couple months old and I hadn't recognized his impact yet. Or maybe it did, and I didn't recognize it. I was young.

For me, normal shifted shortly after the age of four. I know that some people will say a four-year-old has very little cognizant memory (if any memory at all) and many of my stories are incomplete tapestries made-up of pieces of events I heard. But one thing I can say for sure is that the details around this particular event are forever crystallized in my memory and perfectly clear.

Can I tell you what happened the days or weeks before in detail? I cannot. But, in regard to the following event, I can recall some of the smallest details despite my age.

CHAPTER 2

The Icy Pond

Winter in rural Missouri is a lot of fun when you're a kid. It renews everything you have already explored and investigated and starts anew. The ground is different, the trees change, there are snowmen, snow forts, snowball fights, and sledding for hours on end. We also ice skated on the small pond by our house.

Now, I have to admit, I don't love skating. I still don't. But as kids living in a rural area, you are often told to go outside and play, so that's exactly what we did, and we made the best of it.

Despite the cold, Mom would bundle each one of us up so tightly that we could barely bend at the joints. Our arms and legs stuck out like pointy sticks jutting out of a snowman. We were sent out there barely mobile, and it was about an acre and a half away from the main house. The baby – Matt- was too young to go at the time, but the four of us would go with great anticipation.

Paul was the oldest. At that time, he was fourteen—and oh how we looked up to him. Paul was the bravest child out of the bunch. Of course, he was Dad's right-hand-man! And being that he was also the oldest, he was always the first one to test the ice before the rest of us could skate.

We were still getting dressed when he came running back into the house and proclaimed, "It's all good! We can skate!" This assured us that we could go. So, we started rushing to finish getting ready and head outside.

Moments later I burst out the door and made my way toward the pond, trying to keep up with my brothers and sisters.

Before reaching the bank, I paused, so I could put on my skates. Mary, who was 11 at the time, and Susan, who was 9, helped me tie my skates before helping me up to my feet.

"We'll be right here!" Mary said, pointing to the middle of the pond with her mittens. Then, the older kids jetted off to play together.

Finally, I was standing at the edge of the pond, but I could barely move by myself with those heavy skates on, let alone attempt to maneuver successfully.

Other than the occasional fall (or near fall), I was on the edge of boredom before long. I was watching everyone else and was just trying to stay content taking the scene in for a moment.

I witnessed the snow as it blew across the pond and gathered near the edge of the grass. My nose was cold and running furiously. I watched for several minutes, and then the anticipation of joining the crew got the best of me. I could no longer take it.

"I'm bored!" I yelled.

"You're fine! Just play over there!" Susan yelled back at me.

Paul jetted back toward me and checked me over like a paratrooper getting ready for a jump. He looked me dead in the eyes then up and down. He tugged at my coat as if to ensure there were no kinks in my armor.

"Are you cold?" Paul said worriedly.

"No, I'm okay."

"Skate's okay?"

"Yes."

"Gloves?"

"Yes. I'm just bored," I added in between sniffles.

Mary skated over.

"C'mon, David. Try and skate! Here, put your foot sideways like this and push," she said, demonstrating the proper technique.

She finally pivoted, then turned back toward me, grabbing one side, and then Paul grabbed the other side to keep me from falling as we skated out onto the pond together.

It wasn't long before I got enough of a push to move forward a bit.

"Good! Good! Now try again," Mary replied. "You're getting it."

I was excited, I was finally joining them. But it was short lived.

"Oh, he'll never get it," Susan yelled from the center of the pond.

"Shush! He will!" Paul shouted back. "Just keep trying. We will be right here if you need us."

I was bound and determined to skate successfully on my own at that point—not because I liked skating, as I said. I still do not like skating. But something deep inside me was swelling up. I just wanted to be like the other kids who were older than me and bigger and better at skating.

So, I tried again and again, as the other siblings slowly played together in the center of the pond, leaving me to myself.

I was struggling to get movement and getting frustrated. Before long, I was back to boredom again and that inner passion I had to prove the other kids wrong was subsiding.

I could barely stand let alone move. Susan was right, I figured, I was never going to get it. I was rapidly losing faith in my abilities to do anything that involved a pair of skates.

My siblings kept playing and laughing.

I finally noticed a stick that was frozen and sticking halfway up through the ice. I knew that if I could get that stick, I would at least have something to play with while the others continued to skate together, and I wouldn't feel so alone anymore.

Maybe I could even use it like a cane to keep me from falling? Or, I thought, I could use it like a boat's ore and push myself along.

A few moments later, I was inching closer and reached out.

It was just beyond my mitts.

I stretched a little more, almost falling. Once I regained my balance, I stretched once more, and my mitts landed on as my face lit up with pride.

I immediately gave it a good tug—but nothing.

My glove slipped on the stick, and I almost fell backward. Then it occurred to me: my gloves are the problem, I thought.

So, frustrated, I took off my gloves, shoved them in my pocket, and reached toward the stick.

I tugged again. Nothing. I tugged once more. Still nothing.

But I wasn't going to let that stop me. I was going to get that damn stick free from the ice and have something to play with. So, I mustered every bit of courage I had, placed my frozen, red fingers back around the end of the stick, gripped it tightly, then gave one more tug with all I had.

I pulled with every ounce of my strength as the stick finally started to loosen and break free from the ice. Just then, the ground around me started to give.

The ice cracked, and I was in serious trouble.

Paul had the hearing of an owl because he instantly recognized what was happening as the ice continued to crack and give way.

I still remember him yelling out to me as I slid downward.

"Stop!" was all he could get out of his mouth. But I was too fixated on the stick to pay any attention to him.

I freed the stick, but the ice completely gave way at that point. Before I knew it, there was nothing under my feet, and I plunged into the icy pond.

The breaking of the ice sent out what sounded like a clap of thunder that could be heard for miles.

All my siblings froze in their tracks. Things began to move in slow motion. The lower half of my body was already submerged.

I knew if I could just grab the ice I could pull myself up. But as I grabbed at the edge of the ice it broke free.

The cold water rushed all around me, and my clothes were getting waterlogged and heavier. I was getting pulled further down and there was seemingly nothing I could do to stop it.

Before I knew it, I was looking up through the ice completely submerged. The pain was getting worse. My body was tense as if I was going to explode from the inside-out.

My eyeballs hurt with the icy, cold water rushing all around them. I struggled to see anything but shapes and shadows. I wanted to close them, but that left darkness and no chance for me. I struggled to keep them open despite the pain.

I noticed some blurred movements through the ice.

I tried to hold my breath, but the cold water was jabbing at me. I ended up coughing and gagging as the water rushed into my throat—and lungs.

I was in more pain than I've ever experienced before or since.

The fuzzy shapes started slowly disappearing. Blackness followed. Everything was deafly quiet.

No more cold.

No more water.

No more weight of my clothes on my tensed up body.

It took a while, but there was the sound of wind that told me I might be alive.

Instantly, I looked around.

I was just above the fray floating haphazardly.

The pond was beneath me. I was slowly regaining consciousness. The girls came back into focus, and they were stunned by everything happening. Paul was yelling and banging on the ice at something below.

There was something in the water just beneath the surface, but I couldn't make out what it was.

I looked down at the frozen pond again then over at the woods off in the distance an then at our house.

I finally started hearing the faint sound of screams that were getting louder and louder.

Paul and the girl were in a frenzy and yelling in the general direction of something below the surface.

"What's going on?" Mary yelled.

"David fell through," Paul snapped.

"Oh God!" Mary screamed.

"Shut up!" Paul yelled, trying to gain some sense of control over the situation, as he banged at the ice, which had now moved over this thing floating in the water.

Barely cognizant, I kept watching the whole scene as it unfolded.

An object floated near the top of the ice near Paul who was grasping desperately with his arm's outstretched.

The thought never occurred to me at that time. But the thing he was clawing for was me.

I was floating beneath the surface lifeless.

It just didn't feel like me. It felt like a discarded candy wrapper, something I had no attachment to at all.

Now, the thought of that horrified me, and I tried to yell, but I could not form the words.

After beating at the ice, Paul finally switched gears and chose a new tactic.

Unconcerned about his own safety he hopped right in and started pushing against the ice from underneath while beating it from the top; to be clear; the pond was shallow, but just deep enough at my small stature to drown).

As he busted the ice, my body moved further away.

Finally, he hopped out and directed the girls to get Mom. They took off toward the house, and I remember watching as they started the long trek home.

As they ran, the house got smaller and smaller in the background as if it was moving further away. They must have ran for what felt like ten minutes or more, although I know it couldn't have been that long.

Paul was left behind sitting on the ice, shaking his head, trying to catch his breath. Apparently, he had no clue what to do at that point and was losing hope.

In frustration, he started kicking at the ice with his skate. Then he stopped. Then he did it some more. He scooted himself closer to the already broken ice and began chipping away at it. A large chuck gave way near me pushing me deeper under the ice. He stopped and slowly scooted toward it.

Finally, a big wedge broke free, and he fell into the water, too.

"Oh, no. Paul!" I tried to scream, but my words were stuck inside me and couldn't escape.

Before I knew it, he surfaced and was dragging something along behind him.

For a moment, I felt like I was saved! But for some reason, I was still watching the whole scene take place from above and felt disconnected from whatever the thing was that he was tugging.

He was out of breath but kept tugging until he succeeded in reaching the shoreline where he laid the mass down on the frozen ground.

Slowly, he gathered his strength, and his voice got louder and louder.

"David! David!" he screamed.

He was nudging me like he was trying to wake me up from a deep sleep.

I felt nothing.

I wasn't cold or anything. I was nothing. There was no pain, no feeling of clothes on my arms and legs, and I cannot honestly tell you whether or not I had consciously taken a breath in a long time.

I continued to watch as Paul yelled at this seemingly lifeless body he thought was me. It was laying oddly on the cold ground. It wasn't real. It wasn't me. I wondered to myself, how could he think that was me?

I am here, I thought.

A commotion near the house grabbed my attention. The girls had reached the house, and I could hear them yelling as they opened the door.

"David! David! Wake up!" Paul screamed.

Paul picked me up and begin to carry me toward the house. I watched my head slumped back and my mouth was wide open, aghast. My arms, hands, and head bobbed up and down with each step as Paul rushed me toward the house.

Was that me? I don't look like that! I wondered.

I'm here. Right here, I struggled to say, but the words wouldn't materialize physically.

Finally, Paul rushed me inside the house, and I continued to move with him but always above, observing.

It was as if the ceiling was invisible to me because it felt like I was about ten or so feet above the action of the scene, and I could see everything clearly.

"What happened?" Mom shouted as we made it through the door.

Paul didn't answer he just kept moving.

The girls watched in shock as I passed by in Paul's arms. The baby was still sitting in a pumpkin seat on the table. Mom touched my face briefly to check me.

"Get him to the bathroom!" she said, pulling my clothes off as they moved down the hall. All the color had left my skin. I looked a grey-purple color.

They plopped me down into the bathtub and I immediately slumped down to one side. Mom struggled to hold me up with one hand. With the other, she began running hot water over my body, trying to revive me.

Paul collapsed onto the toilet soaking wet and out of breath.

"He's in shock! We have got to get his body temperature up," she cried.

I was still above fray, but I was a little bit closer to the action than before. I noticed my head slumped back at an odd angle and thought to myself that couldn't possibly be me.

I mean, to be fair, it looked kind of like me. It was like a bad, wax museum reproduction of me. But it no uncertain terms was that me, I figured.

I'm here. I'm here! I tried to tell them, but they couldn't hear me, and they kept tending to this slender, lifeless, grey body slumped over in the tub.

Mom tried unsuccessfully to pull more of my clothes off. She took a washcloth and dipped it in the warm water and wiped my face while she yelled at me to respond.

Paul was slumped over the toilet with the water dripping to the cold tile floor below. *Poor Paul,* I thought briefly. No one was helping him, I noticed. And he was just as wet and cold as I was.

The girls stood at the door watching, wondering, weeping, uncertain, fearful.

The once frantic energy had slowly slipped out of the room until only the sound of water filling the bathtub could be heard. Mom looked at me and in a whisper she said, "He's gone."

Just then she started sobbing uncontrollably.

I still recall hearing the silence of nothing but the water filling the tub and my mother's sobs which were muffled and faint.

What seemed like a minute passed as they sat around me trying to grasp things. I tried to grasp things.

What just happened? I was gone? No, I wasn't gone, I thought. *I'm right here. Look at me! Mom! I am right here,* I thought.

I was conscious but still having trouble manifesting any tangible words or maybe the words weren't important. I don't know. Maybe it was just for me to watch and observe, and that's precisely what I was doing.

I felt a pain rising up in my chest that was at first pretty mild. Then it hit me like I was going to puke. This sharp, burning sensation permeating from my insides wanting to come out.

And, it did. I puked violently and started struggling for air. I remember thinking to myself, *I've got to breathe. I need air! Just breath damn it!*

But each breath was more painful than the last.

My eyes finally opened, and I remember my mother's face with this shocked look staring back at me. I was still in the tub. The warm water was rushing over me, and the air was starting to fill my lungs.

Oh, but the pain. It was unbearable. Yet, it was the pain that told me I was alive.

But how? Why? I had so many questions. I still do.

In the pure joy of breathing I concentrated on that one thing and let everything else fade away.

There was puke in the tub, my nose was running everywhere. I had no energy. I hurt all over. I couldn't lift my head on command. That's also right about when the tears started to manifest.

I cried and cried. Oh my God, how I cried that day. It was like a damn wall had been lifted, and the rushing waters filled me limp, near-lifeless arms and limbs.

The shame of the whole situation started to slip in, as well. I was ashamed of what happened. I was ashamed of lying there half naked, completely exposed to everyone, drenching wet, clinging to life. I was also scared of getting into trouble because it happened, and I was probably right.

I wasn't even dry yet before Paul starting blaming everything on me.

"Why did you pull that stick?"

I stood there as Mom rubbed me dry with a rough towel, and her tears were falling on my face. I couldn't even manage to look at her in the face, so I stared down at my toes, wiggling them occasionally to remind myself that I was alive.

I finally let out a soft moan, the first noises I had mustered in I don't know how long.

"Oh, no. Are you hurting?" Mom asked. She seemed genuinely worried.

"No, towel," I replied, still barely able to talk.

"You know you shouldn't have done that!" Susan parroted from just beyond the door.

"Let him be. He is hurt badly!" Mary injected.

"Okay, okay! Let your brother rest. Everyone, go take off your clothes and change. Now!" Mom ordered.

Paul slowly got up from the toilet and made his way out of the bathroom. His clothes were still dripping wet, and he had a confused, worried look on his face as if he just knew he was about to take the heat for the whole thing.

Thank God Dad isn't home, I thought.

I was standing there a pitiful mess. But I was glad to be back in the safety of my home.

Mom continued rubbing on me with that rough, dry towel, and my whole body hurt. I could barely stand. A mixture of pond water, snot, bathwater, and tears dripped onto the floor and collected into a small pool at the base of my bare feet.

I was home with my mother, brothers, and sisters. They could hear me, see me, talk to me, and be mad at me, pretty much all at once, but I was home. I was alive.

I somehow survived.

Then Mom informed me that she was going to call Dad and a knot formed in the back of my throat.

"Well, come to think of it," she said. "There's no need to worry him right now," she added, and the knot slowly dissipated.

She stopped drying me off, dropped the towel, and then grabbed my arms and gently shook me, halfway mad, halfway relieved I had survived.

She knew how close things had gotten.

"You're fine, right?" she asked, more to herself than anyone.

I shook my head and mustered a small grin.

Just like that it was if it never happened. We all tried to push it as far out of our minds as possible. I don't mean there were some minor discussions. I mean, it was twenty years before we, as siblings, discussed what happened that day in any form whatsoever. It wasn't the only thing we never talked about. It was a family habit not to discuss certain events.

But I will never forget my experiences with that icy pond that cold wintry day.

Was it near death?

Was I dead but came back to life? And if so, Why? How?

I still don't know today. But I'll never forget watching the entire scene unfold while watching above the fray, wondering why no one could hear my pleas and why I felt so disconnected from that purple-grey mass.

I couldn't grasp why no one was listening to me—and why everyone seemed so concerned with that crumpled up, frail, grey-little body they were calling David over and over. It made no sense to me.

Of course, I eventually came to accept that the lifeless mass was me in some form, which was a pivotal moment in my young life. That whole event would help to define my life in ways that I can never fully explain. I knew about Christianity. I was taught about God and that people sometimes die. But, for me, that one event confirmed there was more to life and more to what we knew about life.

That's not to say I don't still have questions. Where was I? Why was I? How was I? And, most of all, why don't people talk about that kind of stuff?

You would think it would be Christianity 101. The chapter that covers freaky shit that will change your life forever. But it's not. In fact, mostly, we are taught that death is the end of things for the most part. Or, we're taught that we must go to our graves until the day Christ returns and we can meet our maker in the sky somewhere above. And, still yet, some religions do not talk about those sort of things at all.

I guess I've just never really understood why religions do not try to answer one of the biggest questions in life.

What the hell happens after death?

Wouldn't you like to know? Wouldn't you like to study the issue, have the discussion, and see where it leads?

Maybe it's just me. But I don't understand any of that to this day. There's no inquisitiveness when it comes to life after death. For me, it is events like the one I went through that should support most spiritual and religious beliefs. To not discuss them at all seems like a major oversight—or worse.

It would be like a prosecutor throwing out THE single piece of evidence that supports their entire case along with the witness to go along with that evidence just to prove some vague notion they may have about something else entirely. It is illogical at best, criminal at worst.

Yet, that's exactly what happens every single day in households, churches, schools, and beyond in this world.

For me, the icy pond incident would become a blessing and a curse. From the tender age of four, it solidified there is something beyond this physical world. So, for years, I have known for a fact that there is more to this life than what we see and discuss. Just as sure as the sky is blue, I know. That event was also the proof a higher power exists.

Unfortunately, the one rock solid confirmation that a high power exists is the one thing most Christians choose not to accept or talk about. In fact, instead of ignoring that aspect of faith they go one step further. They shun and disapprove such notions.

At age four I couldn't grasp it, as you can imagine. Nor have I completely grasped it all since that time, but it's something I've pondered a great deal.

My experience did one more thing for me, too. People that have known me my entire life tend to say I have no fear. They may be right. Now, it's not in the "he's an idiot" or "he'll do anything" mold. It's that I have no fear of failure, no fear to hold onto preconceived beliefs, and no fear to live my life how I see fit according to my own terms.

I credit that one event to feeding my soul and putting me on the right path at an early age. Other events throughout my life would ensure I stayed the course and keep me nourished.

I call those events confirmations, and my life is full of them. Confirmations are paranormal tattoos on the soul, and you can choose to accept them and wear them like a badge of honor. That's how I live my life. Of course, it wasn't always that way.

At some point along the way, a "liar" was born. Allow me to explain.

CHAPTER 3

A Liar is Born

The rest of the week was a blur. In typical fashion, I never went to the hospital or doctor. No ambulance was called. I don't think I even missed school, although we probably had more than one snow day off regardless.

After several rounds of cough and cold meds, I was declared "all better" by my mother. I recall feeling almost detached from the things going on around me, almost out-of-body.

Pretty soon, the weekend came, so Dad was home again. Dad definitely ruled the roost, at least during those years. When the story of me drowning did come up, it was in casual conversation by Mom. It was a light and breezy conversation (completely downplayed). I never knew if she did that for his sake, for hers, or for ours.

They were sitting at the kitchen table. It was pretty early in the morning, and none of the other kids were up yet. I snuck my way up the hall and cautiously approached them until they finally acknowledged me. I was hoping they would not send me back to bed.

"Hey, little guy," my father said when he saw me. "Come sit on my lap and have some breakfast with me."

He grabbed me with his vast catcher's mitt hands and placed me on his lap that seemed like a couch to me. Dad fed me little bits of his omelet while my mother caught him up on the week's events. Then it was my turn.

"What has David been up to?" he asked, smiling down at me.

I was hesitant to even answer. I didn't know what to say or not say—and I was temporarily frozen.

"It's ok. Tell me what happened," he added.

I started feeling more at ease.

"I went skating," I finally replied, albeit hesitantly at first.

"You did?" he sarcastically replied and began to look at my mother.

"Oh, Cline. The kids went out," My mother immediately interjected.

My father gave her a look.

She stopped talking.

He looked back down at me, the stern look he gave Mother fading slowly away.

"I fell down," I said and paused.

"You did? You're gonna do that a lot before you learn not to fall," he replied.

I looked up at his big eyes staring back at me. I had to tell him.

"No, I fell down and—"

Before I could finish, my mother interrupted again.

"He fell and broke the ice. He was so cold and disoriented that Paul had to carry him up to the house. They got here and made an awful mess. I had to get on them and make them change and clean up right away before they brought that mess through the house."

She was talking so fast and nervously that I think it took Father by surprise, as well.

I was feeling pretty odd at that point and couldn't figure out why Mom was downplaying what happened.

Why was she doing that? I wondered. Why is Dad just calmly looking down at me?

"Well, little guy. One day you'll learn how to ice skate. So, don't quit trying. No one starts without falling down every now and then. Okay?" he added.

I shook my head.

"Okay," he replied, patting the top of my head, which must have disappeared under his meaty paw.

He exhaled deeply, then grabbed me by my arms and picked me up, placing me on the floor beside him.

"Let me and Mom chat a little bit," he said. "Go play in the front room, okay?"

I shook my head, adding, "Yes, Dad."

I then bolted from the room.

I can only imagine the conversation that took place once I left. My father was a sage. He was a very perceptive man, even way back then.

I know even though they tried to talk quietly, his voice was getting louder and louder.

I froze up at one point as his powerful voice echoed through the house. Dad must have put two and two together with me falling, the ice breaking, and us being wet. He must have suspected that things had gotten worse than he was being led to believe—and didn't like that he was being misled.

There was one thing Dad never liked. He didn't want his kids at risk of being hurt.

Apparently, Mom had gotten caught trying to minimize the situation, and he didn't like it.

As I mentioned before, my parents had very different belief systems when it came to religion (and pretty much everything else). This event didn't help to bridge that divide in the least. Nothing demonstrated that gap more than the way they reacted to my experience or the resulting struggles I had trying to cope with the aftermath of the experience.

I struggled a lot with what happened, ranging from not wanting to go back outside to not wanting to talk about it.

Dad came home the next weekend, and I was anxious to talk to him. If anyone could understand what happened and answer my questions, it was Dad.

So, I waited until he was alone in the front room in his chair on Saturday and snuck in to speak with him.

"Dad?" I said, slowly approaching.

"What's on your mind, little guy?" he said, plopping me down on his lap.

Dad patiently waited as I struggled to talk. Before I knew it, I was tearing up.

"I don't wanna die!" I finally yelled, crying.

He wrapped me in his huge arms and hugged me.

"You don't need to worry about dying," he assured me.

"But I drowned," I eked out between the tears.

I felt my father take in a deep breath and pause. It was if the weight of that hitting him. Or maybe it was the truth of it that finally hit him. He hugged me tighter.

After a long silence, he replied softly, "And it scared you?"

I shook my head.

"You don't need to worry. Did you know your body is not you?"

I was too upset to answer, but I shook my head no. I had no clue what he was talking about.

My body is me, I thought.

Who else am I? I wondered.

"Your body is just a shell. Like the seeds in the garden. They have a shell that eventually goes away so the plant can grow. You are like that seed. And you are tucked safely away inside the shell. You," he said, pausing. "Are a soul."

"A soul is who you are. But it is not physical. We have to have a body. So, your soul rides along in your body like we do when our bodies ride along in a car. But we're not the car. We're inside the car just like your soul is inside you," he continued.

My father always had the best analogies that seemed to cut right through to the crux of whatever we were discussing.

I was completely perplexed and had so many questions. Yet this somehow made sense to me and put my whole experience in a better light. It was exactly what I needed to hear. It was comforting because, otherwise, I was terribly afraid of dying after the incident.

But I had supreme confidence in my father. He went on to explain what he meant by a soul and then remained patient to answer all of my questions.

"Where do we go when we die?" I finally asked.

My father opened up to me more than he had ever done before. He discussed his own personal beliefs and assured me that there was no need to worry about death at all because we never really die.

At that point, I was feeling a lot better than I had in a long time. By the time we stopped talking, I felt confident enough to no longer fear death even if I didn't understand all the details of what we were discussing.

Then, Susan entered the room and approached us.

"My turn to sit on Dad's lap!" she said.

My father kissed me on my forehead as I slid off his lap.

"So, what is Susie been up to?"

I left the room as their voices faded away in the background.

However, the words he had left with me continued to reverberate through my mind. All of a sudden, I felt comfortable and confident. And because of the renewed confidence, I was finally able to start talking about what actually happened to me when I drowned.

Over the following week, while the older kids were at school, my mother, younger brother, and I attended some Bible studies courses.

. . .

WE WERE sitting in a circle at a fellow member's home. I was a reasonably quiet kid, so typically, I wouldn't engage with other people vocally. I was more content sitting on the floor and playing while the other adults held Bible study.

However, I had been listening more intently than I usually would. The subject was baptism. Maybe it was the water, or people going under the water, or maybe it was about being renewed. Something grabbed my attention and resonated with me.

Finally, I blurted out, "I drowned!"

"What dear?" one personal replied.

"I drowned!" I repeated proudly.

"You what dear?" a lady questioned.

"I drowned. I went under the ice and drowned. Then, I watched…"

I stopped speaking as a foreboding feeling washed over me. You know that feeling when you are at a concert or blaring music and the vibrations hit your skin and you feel like you are shaking straight to the core? In those Moments, your skin feels tingly to the touch as if all the receptors were on high alert.

I remember the look on the lady's face and a commotion in the group as the words spilled out of my mouth and into the room.

Mom quickly noticed the stir my words were causing and had a response as she picked me up.

"Oh, David, what are you saying?" she asked me. "You know he has stories about everything. He just rattles on since he started talking," she informed everyone else.

"No!" I yelled back at her. It was clear to me she had no idea what really happened. Probably because we never talked about it!

"I drowned!" I repeated.

I felt like if Mom didn't believe maybe others would. Dad seemed to.

Everyone was still in shock. It was not just at my words, or at what I was saying happened, or the fact they never heard anything about my drowning, but the fact I dared to yell back at her.

At four years old I did not realize the weight of the situation I now found myself in but continued forward nonetheless

"I drowned. I watched Paul carry as I watched him from the sky." I said. "That's what happened, and I remember it." The sensation was now ringing in my ears intensely.

"Now, David. Stop it! You're lying!" Mom quickly said, covering my mouth to stop me.

I couldn't believe what was happening.

I knew what happened. I told Dad what happened. He had made me more comfortable with the whole situation—and my mortality. And now there's my own mother calling me a liar.

Looking back, that was another one of those pivotal Moments in my young life, almost as pivotal as the drowning itself.

One of the elderly women in the group had an opinion to give next.

"You know it is not a good sign that he is taking to lying at such a young age! The devil has a hold on him," she cautioned my mom.

My face must have been blood red.

No one was believing me, so I screamed into my mother's hand as she cupped her palm tightly over my mouth. Definitely, I tried to wiggle my head free and scream some more, but her grip merely tightened, nearly cutting off all my air.

She was bound and determined to shut me up, as her face grew beet red, matching my own expression.

"You are so right," my mother said, standing. You know, it's really amazing, but she had somehow managed to cover my mouth as she struggled to gather her things along with my brother in the pumpkin seat.

"It's … well, it's my husband. He is filling their heads with all kinds of wild things. You know he is not one of us!" she said as if she were ashamed of who my dad was, and that really upset me.

What she should have said was that he wasn't in their religion and didn't believe like them. But in their minds, anyone who wasn't one of them was 100% wrong. About everything. No matter what. The case was closed as far as they were concerned, and there was no use talking about it.

Their little sect represented one side of the divide—and everyone else who strayed away from their message was inevitably on the other side even if it was a family member or friend. Doesn't matter. It's an us versus them mentality that's so pervasive in many religious sects.

"He has not found the TRUTH yet. But I pray. I pray he does every single day," she assured them. "I pray he comes into the light, quits lying, and recognizes the wickedness of his ways."

At that point, we were heading out of the circle to the nearest exit. I was being pulled with one hand. She had miscellaneous other items in her other arm. My brother was still in the pumpkin seat. She was dropping things along the way, trying to get out the door as fast as possible, all the while her face was glowing red with embarrassment and shame.

Oh, I had done it this time. I knew it too. I was in big trouble, and all my anger at being called a liar had transitioned to fear and anxiety. I wondered what was going to happen to me once we left— but shuttered at the mere thoughts of it.

"You need to watch the grip the devil has on that one already," someone else added as we backed away.

"He's becoming a liar," another one chimed in.

I looked at the passing eyeballs as their words bounced off me one by one.

"I am. I mean, I do, brothers and sisters. I do! Let me take him outside and have a talk with him. I'll get him straightened out."

We exited out the door, and it immediately closed behind us. She finally sat my brother down, dropped her things, and then headed for my general direction.

Here it comes. No hiding. I tried to muster my courage as she yanked my arm with one hand and then started swatting me as hard as she could with the other.

Bam! Bam! Bam! Over and over, she repeated the motions, slapping my backside with the open palm of her hand. With each blow, a sharp sting went through my limbs. I tried to hold it in, but it was no use as I cried out and the tears streamed down my face.

I don't know how long the whipping lasted, but it felt like several minutes. Fortunately, before long, my butt became numb to the strokes.

I didn't really understand what it was that I did wrong, but they certainly felt like I had done something.

To me, I was just trying to tell everyone what happened. I did drown. I did see everything clearly from up above the fray. It was the truth. What's wrong with that?

After exhausting herself, she finally sat me down on the porch to discuss some things with me. Tears were still rolling down my cheeks as she spoke, and I brushed them aside as I stared up at her.

"David Christopher," she said. The mere fact she used my first AND middle name was indication of how terrible the situation was. "Look, you cannot lie about things. It's not right."

"I wasn't Mom."

"You cannot tell stories and pass them off as truth."

"I'm not telling a story. I'm not. I—"

"You are!" she snapped. "You were lying right in front of all those people about things that are not true, and now you're continuing to lie to me!"

I had heard all I could take. My butt was still numb, but I had heard enough.

"I am not lying!" I screamed at the top of my lungs.

She stopped in shock. She wasn't used to any of her children talking back.

"Do you need another whipping?"

"No!"

"Then don't you ever disrespect me by yelling at me. And don't you fib like that again! Do you understand?"

Part of me wanted to say, "Yes. I understand."

But I couldn't.

"I am not lying!"

She'd reply, "You are lying."

Finally, she stopped mid-sentence and looked at me. She was completely shocked. It finally occurred to me that not only was I not lying but that she was the one who was actually lying.

She knew what happened, too. She was there.

"You're lying," I blurted out.

It did not take her long to reply after a deep breath.

"Now mister you cannot—"

"You're lying," I repeated.

She paused.

"And why do you say that mister smarty pants?"

I proudly replied, "Because I was there!"

There was a rush as I said it. I was finally admitting what had happened. My skin tingled when I said it.

"I saw it all!" I proudly exclaimed. "And you gave up on me."

I don't know what response I expected but a smack across the mouth was not it. The impact—or maybe it was the surprise of the impact—sent me to the ground.

I landed hard. When I gathered my wits, she was staring down over me like a schoolhouse bully.

"Now, you listen to me!" she demanded. "I am sick of your lies and your story about what happened. You are going to go back in there and apologize for lying, and then you are going to come out here and do your studies alone. Do you understand me?"

I was stunned by the backhand and didn't move an inch. The rush I felt from speaking the truth started to subside. A different, darker sensation came over me. This was a new feeling.

Dark, uncomfortable. My lips fattened.

"Yes, Mom," I said begrudgingly.

She picked me up, dusted me off, and proudly marched me back into the study circle to apologize as if she was presenting a gift to the pack.

I lied that day. I did not state exactly what happened but what she wanted me to say happened. What I told them that day was a lie, and it still bothers me. I guess I am a liar!

. . .

AS I SAID before, there were no open discussions in our family concerning the event or what happened after the event for over a decade. At the same time, I was struggling with what was and wasn't real, as well as people's notions of normal.

However, at least for a while, at least for our family, the matter was settled, which is exactly how our family dealt with a lot of things, at least until us siblings got old enough (and wise enough) to know better.

For years we were led to believe that the best way to handle our problems was to avoid them (and not discuss them) in the first place.

So, that's exactly what happened for a very long time.

As far as the sensations, they were different for different situations. It took me some time to accept those sensations much less relate them to a specific situation.

I knew by age four or five that simply understanding the sensations were inconceivable to many people, especially my mother and her religious friends. For me, they were just something that would happen sometimes.

It took a long time before I would be able to tie them to any specific situation. And it took even longer to be able to ascribe any sort of meaning to those situations.

Shortly after the incident with my mother, I became a much quieter child altogether. In fact, my siblings have even said that I basically stopped talking to everyone. I just threw up a wall and hid inside somewhere.

I think the truth is that I was just questioning a lot of things and grappled with truth, reality, and normalcy. In addition, I was struggling with how telling the truth could also be considered a lie. I never knew how people would react when I talked. It was just easier to keep my mouth shut.

In hindsight, maybe I even believed her. Maybe I was a liar. In her mind and in the minds of her religious friends, I certainly was a liar.

I also had the devil in me, apparently. Or that is what the adults said.

When I would talk it was to myself in a whisper and when someone entered the room, I would clam up and shut down entirely. Things got so bad they were ready to have me tested and threatened that I could not start kindergarten until I talked.

But what should I have talked about?

I wasn't taking well to being called a liar—or being told that I had the devil acting through me.

I imagine that sort of thing wouldn't sit well with most children, and yet that was my reality.

I know now that people often struggle confronting the gravity of certain experiences. But, for me, it was my own mother who gave me my first taste of not accepting my experiences. She even saw what I had said as a threat toward her entire way of life. It was a contradiction to her religious beliefs and that was blasphemous!

It was my start down the path of being branded a liar and that was a hard lesson, especially being so young. And truth escaped me. If saying what happened wasn't the truth, then what was?

Do you really believe that people want to know the truth? Or, are they content with some other reality that's not exactly the truth?

In popular psychology, there's another meaning of denial, which is a psychological defense we all use at times to reduce our anxiety when something feels disturbing or makes us uncomfortable.

But the truth is absent in that equation.

We get uncomfortable and immediately shut down even if what's making us uncomfortable is true and needs to be confronted.

When seemingly intelligent and sane adults vehemently deny truths despite a body of irrefutable data, it should really make us all stop and give pause.

We won't go too far down that rabbit hole, but I think it's safe to say that avoiding truth because we're uncomfortable with it is not sufficient enough reason to reject it altogether.

I knew that if I mentioned anything regarding my experience, I'd be ostracized or worse. Meanwhile, I struggled with all the anxiety that came from having to accept a different reality from what I believed to be true. For the moment, it left me confused and wondering what truth really was.

CHAPTER 4
Changes

It was immediately obvious that the experience I had while drowning was more than just a physical one. There soon came a whole host of other unusual experiences that left me questioning and dealing with a lot more than expected. I still do not know to this day if that experience opened a door for me, or other events in my life caused things to occur more rapidly.

Maybe the door was already open, and I just found it. Or maybe I invited things in at that point. I only know that things begin to change for me concerning my family and on the spiritual front.

On occasion, I would even see things or know certain outcomes or details before they occurred There was no logical explanation for how I knew those things to be true. There was no possible way I could have known what was going to happen—and yet I did.

I have talked to psychologists who felt like children had the bad habit of seeing or hearing things and not realizing they were seeing or hearing them. They use this rational for explaining how people can see or know things before they happen. But, while I think that may sometimes be the case, there have been things that occurred in my life that have me questioning whether it's always true.

In my mind, the experiences were clearly new, clearly not from me, and clearly from someone or something else. There were times as a child that I felt such an energetic stimulus in the air that my hair would literally stand on end, and I would get goosebumps from head toe. That is not because of something I had somehow heard or saw previously without knowing it. I actually think that logic falls all apart once you really think about it, which I have repeatedly tried to make sense of since that time.

Another undeniably strange experience occurred when I woke up in the middle of the night with everything deafly silent. I had been in a dead sleep when an all new sensation became evident.

From the inside, the moon gently lit my room where I could barely make out anything but shapes and shadows in the darkness. Instantly, my mind was drawn to something outside as if compelling me to look in that general direction.

As I stared out the window, a bright silhouette of a figure appeared just beyond my window from the other side. It was what could best be described as a human-like or angelic figure, but the details are hard to describe because it was so bright that I could barely cast my eyes upon it for more than a second or two.

Was I dreaming? Absolutely not. Like I said, I felt compelled to wake up and investigate what was happening.

From the window, I squinted to see what it was as a rush of fear hit me. But no matter how scared I was, I dared not to scream and wake up Mom or Dad. Besides, who would ever believe a liar anyway?

So, it was just me—and whatever that thing was.

I knew it was something I needed to face on my own—so I did the only thing I knew how to do.

Questions ran through my child mind. Who or what was it? What does it want? What's it doing there? Does it see me? Is it trying to tell me something? Or, does it want to hurt me?

The little hairs on my frail arms stood in rapt attention. I had goosebumps in places I didn't' know you could get goosebumps. And a huge knot formed in the back of my throat, and try as I might, I couldn't swallow it down.

It's like I was all of the sudden suffocating. I clasped at my throat, but it was useless. All the breaths had escaped me.

This being of light was so blinding, I looked away.

Then, I tried to squint and make out what it was from the corner of my eyes.

So far, it was standing still and calm just beyond the window. Not one movement.

I swallowed repeatedly and finally got the huge knot in my throat to go down as the fresh air hit my lungs.

I pulled the covers over my eyes and tried to pretend like it wasn't there, but I knew in my heart it was still there no matter how hard I tried to ignore it.

I still didn't know what it was or what it was doing there. The sensations were hard to describe, but it was an easiness that grips you at your core and won't let go. It's the kind of fear that unless you've felt it is hard to understand. It's heart-stopping terror that I was trying to come to grips with then—and at other times since that time.

I don't know how long I kept the blankets over my eyes, but it seemed to be five, six minutes. Because the blanket was pulled all the way over my head, and I couldn't see it any longer. But I knew it was still there. I could feel it.

I guess I was hoping it would just go away, but somehow, I knew that it wasn't going to. It's like it was stalking me or something.

Finally, I mustered my courage. I pulled the covers back and slowly opened my eyelids and looked out the window once more.

I didn't see it anymore. It was gone.

Then something moved in my room and the brightness was back. My eyes shot to capture it. The figure was now closer.

My heart sank as I realized it was now inside the room with me. I was in fear for my life, and I started to scream out, but the words wouldn't materialize. I was frozen in panic.

What was it? I wondered.

I threw the covers back over my head and clinched my eyes as tight as I could and tried to breathe. In and out. In and out. I just laid there and tried to breathe.

At that point, I couldn't see it, but I could sense it's movement as if it was shifting throughout the room. It darted one last time from across the room to over my bed and then up and out of the room altogether.

As quickly as it had come into my room, it was now gone, and I was completely and utterly speechless.

The experience was as real to me as my mother or father or siblings. I knew it to be true- even if no one else ever would.

I can't say for sure exactly what I saw that night—but I know it was real because I saw it, and more importantly, I felt it.

Looking back, there was no intruder in the house to harm us or rob us. But what was it? I often wonder.

Maybe I fell asleep at some point or just completely imagined the whole thing, but it's hard to imagine that I could possibly create something so detailed in my mind and not realize that I was creating it myself. The most troubling aspect was the fact I couldn't speak about it with anyone.

I had my father who would have been great to talk to, but I had no clue what to say. Plus, as described, I had already been labeled a liar, and I didn't like being called a liar, and I was growing tired of providing people the fuel they could use against me.

After that night, I felt more alone than ever.

Dad never actually questioned or accused me of lying, but I couldn't help but worry if it would somehow become another tale, another story, or another lie that I had somehow spun. Maybe Mom could change his mind? Or maybe the kids would hear and tease me. I ended up not telling anyone until now. This is the first I ever talked about this malevolent being.

. . .

I WAS GOING THROUGH a lot of changes back then, but one thing was a constant—my new friend. It would visit me a lot back then. And like any young child, I was terrified, at least at first.

It was almost as if it knew and stopped entering the room, particularly while I was aware of it. There were times I would see it standing outside my window. It would happen whether it was during the day—or night, so I wasn't dreaming.

Slowly, the weeks went by.

Weeks turned into months.

Visits from this being were becoming less frequent but still happening from time to time. What first became fear at the mere thought of my mysterious visitor eventually gave way to comfort.

I started thinking of these visits as if it was somehow standing guard over me. Maybe it was trying to just say, "I am here. You are safe. I am here to protect and comfort you." That is at least the feeling I eventually got with its presence. I can't say for sure if that was its intent, but that's how I took it because that's how I felt. But what was it protecting me (or us) from?

I never came to really know my visitor anymore that what I've already described. I never came to understand who it was or what it was doing. I would actually love to report that it stayed with me my whole life, but eventually it left, or I lost the ability to see it.

It is hard to say if it's still around today or not. True, occasionally I will get a similar feeling as if it is present. I do believe it was a spiritual being that was with me for some specific reason, but as noted, I'm still unaware of those reasons to this day.

I do, however, credit it with my love of angels, which began during that time.

When I say angels—I don't mean the chubby cherub types from literature, art, and pop culture. I mean angels in the bad ass sense like an Archangel that can fight and instill fear even in the bravest of men or the most formidable of enemies.

Was it an angel? I don't know, but I know that it was spiritual and kind and that it didn't mean to scare me or harm me. I was only fearful at first because it something out of the ordinary to me at the time. We tend to fear things that they do not understand.

While I still do not fully understand who my visitor was, I do have the keen sense that it was a spiritual being whose bright light and helped to get me through some of my darkest, loneliest, most trying times as a child. It's presence comforted me.

And, as if that was not strange enough, the experiences I endured with my visitor were not isolated.

. . .

DURING THAT TIME period, I was also having what I call my "Running Man dreams."

On one particular night, my family was riding along in our car. It was getting pretty late, and I was in the backseat, which was the norm. The beams from our headlights cast a bright light across the woods as we passed. I found myself in a trance-like state watching the trees go by over and over again.

Finally, in the dark of night something caught my eye.

It was a yellow-green glow, and it was keeping pace with us in the distance. Then it started getting closer and closer.

What at first looked like a glowing, nondescript blob was coming into shape, and I could finally make out what appeared to be glowing eyes.

At first, I assumed it was some sort of animal. As we kept moving, it just kept getting closer and closer while it moved parallel to the road alongside us.

Was it an animal? How would an animal dart between the trees and still keep up with a speeding car?

As much as I wanted to, I could not break my stare. I was entranced with this thing with its bright, glowing eyes. As it moved closer, even more detail came into view.

It had on some sort of dark tattered poncho or robe. Its skin was ashy and gray. It's fiery green, yellow eyes locked right on me.

Despite it having to somehow dodge trees, it was running or floating between them and continuing to keep perfect pace with our car.

I continued to stare at it, and it was staring right back at me as it got closer and closer. My heart was racing until it was right outside my passenger's side window looking right at me! Not saying a word. Then came the smile. It was showing it's jagged teeth.

I would always wake up screaming from this dream as a child, especially when those vicious teeth came out.

In the months and years that followed, I would see this strange light figure more times than I can count, and it always looked the same. When I see the figure, it gives me a wholly different sensation than when I saw the slightly more benevolent figure from the preceding section.

It always looked the same but never spoke to me.

It would only visit me in my dream state—and I was always terrified of it. It's as if it was also trying to tell me something except this time it wasn't comforting. It didn't come to protect me or lend me comfort.

This spiritual being was far more malevolent, or, at the least, that's the impression it always gave me.

To be honest, I still get that same dream occasionally. I have taught myself not to scream but cannot teach myself with this dream to wake up before it gives it's eerie smile. I've never understood what it means or what it represents.

I just know that I'm terrified when it happens.

. . .

AS IF THINGS weren't changing enough already, the early spring brought even more change to my life in the form of an extraordinary event.

One day, while in the backyard playing with my cars, I heard a faint sound in the distance. My younger brother was nearby playing. I was intent on not being bothered, but then I heard another noise, which was slightly louder than before. It repeated again—and again.

And then out of nowhere I saw a horse in the back of the field. Then I saw two covered wagons behind the horse. But they didn't look anything like the covered wagons you may be familiar with. It was like I was looking at them through a heat signature.

The wagons were wavy and distant, and an elderly man hopped down from one of them and went around the back where he lifted two kids down, a boy and a girl. Another older man and his wife got out of the other wagon.

I could not believe what I was seeing.

I looked at Matt as if to say, "Hey, check this out!"

But he was not even reacting. I looked down at my cars as if to wish it away. When I looked back up the boy and the girl were running around chasing one another.

"Hey," I said to Matt.

Matt looked at me like I was crazy.

"What?"

I pointed at the field. He looked for a minute and paused. Then went back to playing.

He couldn't see them. Was he too young? Or did he just not care? I had no idea.

So, I started playing again and tried to ignore them or at least attempted to. I finally looked up again. By now, they were unpacking their gear from the back of the wagon as if to set up for the night. I didn't know what to do.

Should I say something?

Could they see me?

I tried to play some more, but all the while I was wondering what the heck was going on in the back of the field. I couldn't take my mind off the family of pioneers who whoever they were. When I finally looked back up they were still there but barely visible. I looked back down at my matchbox cars momentarily and then back toward the field and they were gone. The images of the pioneer family had completely faded away.

They were gone, but the images had been etched into my mind, and there was no forgetting what I had witnessed.

In the coming days and weeks, I got to see the kids again, but it always started with the arrival of the same wagon. Moreover, the kids kept working their way closer toward our house. The boy would stand there and just stare at us sometimes. The girl would often wave or smile. But no words were ever spoken. They just stared at us while we played. The adults never seemed to be interested in us at all. Maybe they were too busy, maybe they just didn't care, or maybe they couldn't see us as at all. But the kids certainly could.

I had so many questions, as you can imagine. Who were they? Where did they come from? I would often times try to answer those questions, but every attempt I made to get closer to them or talk with them or play, Mom would catch me and call me back before I could get too close. It's like she had this sixth sense and recognized I was getting too close to danger or something. She would never let us wonder too far from the house, which left me wondering if maybe she knew more than she was letting on.

From time to time, I would anxiously check the backyard and field for the wagons and unknown visitors. When the wagons arrived, they were always in the same place with the same people around the same time of year (early spring or summer). I never once saw them in the fall or winter.

And the adults were always wrapped up with various tasks and payed us no mind at all. The kids? They knew we were there, and it's like they wanted so badly to communicate with us—but couldn't. I know I'm not doing this story justice, but that's how I remember things.

In fact, recalling things now, the adults never really interacted with the boy or the girl either short of lifting out of the wagon. The children were the only ones that changed their activities (or perhaps they were the only ones allowed to do so). Every chance I had I would try to talk to the children.

I would always get in trouble if I tried to wander too far from the house. Sometimes, I would stand at the patio door, nose in the corner, and sneak peaks at the boy and girl who were busy playing. The little girl would sometimes grin and wave at me, inviting me to play with her.

It was sheer torture. And it was during one of those punishments from running off that I anxiously watched the little pioneer kids having fun. In fact, they were having so much fun the they back toward the woods as if they didn't have a care in the world. I still remember trying to recall what it must have been like to feel that free. I also wondered what the "big" woods as we called them must have been like.

One day, I was so taken by all of it that I flung open the door and ran into the backyard despite my grounding.

"Wait! Wait!" I yelled at them." I want to play too!"

As fast I could run in my bare feet, I pursued them. The little girl paused and waved at me, then turned around and quickly disappeared into the tree line with her brother.

The excitement was growing in my chest, and I could barely contain my enthusiasm. My heart was pounding so hard I could feel it in my throat. Was it the running or the pure joy of finally playing along with them?

"David!" Mom yelled, her voice breaking the elation. "Get your butt back here right now."

I stopped dead in my tracks.

I had hoped to disappear within the trees and catch up with my friends before she spotted me, but it was too late.

I was busted.

I looked back at the tree line and took another step toward a small opening in the trees. From my vantage point, I could hear the little kids giggling and playing from inside the trees somewhere. They couldn't have been more than twenty or thirty feet from my exact location, which was the closest I'd ever been to them.

As I took one more step forward, I stopped. Something wouldn't let me move. It's like an invisible force was holding me back not letting me move forward.

"David! David!"

With my heart still pounding in my ears, I could barely hear my mother's faint voice in the background. I looked back at the house then wheeled back toward the tree line. I knew what I had to do.

Today wasn't the day.

"I'm sorry!" I yelled out toward my friends. "I can't come play today. Come to my house and play!"

There was no response from the kids only the faint sounds of their distant laughter, which cut through the warm, humid air like a razor blade.

For a brief moment, I moved toward the trees once more and the slightest notion that I might defy my mother. I wanted more than anything in the world at that exact moment to play with them and have some friends.

It certainly appeared to me that they wanted to play; at least, in my mind, the girl seemed to want to play. She would smile and wave at me all the time. She never spoke, but she had a nice face.

Now, the little boy, her brother I image, would often twist his face or stick out his tongue at me as if to mock me or dare me to come.

I finally made up my mind. I had to get back home before Mom came. Maybe some other day.

"I gotta run!" I yelled and then wheeled back around and started making my way back toward the house.

I could make out my mother's threats of punishment spewing from her mouth as I got closer. My expression turned from excited to sullen.

However, I was bound and determined that I would someday play with my new "friends." I didn't know the time or day. But I felt a closeness to them that I hadn't felt with anyone up until that point if that makes any sense at all, and I prayed deeply that I would get my chance to meet them soon.

In the meantime, there were a number of other things that would succeed at pulling my attention away from the pioneer family and that little girl with the nice face, at least for a spell.

CHAPTER 5
Party Tricks

I was lying on my belly, playing on the living room floor, pushing the little cars across the carpet.

"Vroom! Vroom!" I said just above a whisper while moving the little matchbox cars along the made-up track. The cars sped around the in big sweeping ovals from the force of my tiny hands and over-active imagination.

The police car pulled onto the track from nowhere and flipped his blue lights on.

"Uh, oh. You're in big trouble," he cautioned.

I could almost hear as the siren rang out in my mind, denoting the speedsters had drawn the ire of law enforcement. This wasn't good at all.

"Pull over. Pull over," he echoed, and a tiny grin etched its way across my face. The guilty offender slowed to a crawl as the police officer drew closer.

"I said pull over! You're in big trouble," he warned.

I was completely lost in my own little world when my father came along and plopped down in his chair and started reading from one of his books.

Mom was always reading the Bible, but Dad had a variety of books and spent a great deal of his time reading them.

Of course, when he was reading, I knew better than to bother him. At the same time, I really loved him and looked up to him a lot, so I wanted to be as close to him as possible even if it just meant playing at his feet sometimes.

The truth is, I could probably get away with that sort of thing more than the other kids because I was a lot quieter than the other kids, even when I was playing. And even though I was no longer the baby, I was still pretty young.

So, I contently pushed my cars around close to his feet, which were positioned rather closely to the bookcase.

Oh what a bookcase that was! It was full of wonderful books I only wished I could read—and I don't mean the kind with pictures. Like any child, I liked those, too. But Dad's books had a certain magical quality that's hard to describe.

He had long ago informed us that there were no kids' books in the vicinity. Not only that, his bookshelf was completely off limits to me or the other children, so that made me want to look at them worse than anything.

I finally dropped the police car, apparently letting the speeder off with just a warning.

I started looking at the titles of his many books and was utterly mesmerized. Mom had a few books of her own on top, but they were all from the church or Christian related. Dad's books were below and more visible because most of his were on the two bottom shelves.

They covered a wide range of topics, and I was just now learning to read a little bit and could make out some of the words. I saw some books about history and others that sounded more spiritual. Before long, I came to realize those were his favorites. I could make out words like "occult," "devil," "spiritualism," "unlocking the mind," "beliefs," and some words I couldn't quite make out all the way. Some of them had what looked like burn marks on the edges.

Looking back, that bookcase was a physical representation of my parents and their marriage, Mom being 100% church, Father being spiritual and explorative.

They were two totally different people living two totally separate lives under one roof.

My father realized I was interested in his books, and he called me to sit on his lap. I was happy because it meant I was going to get some up close time with him.

"The Indians believed you could leave your body and travel great distances. Did you know that?"

I shook my head.

I did not know that.

He was staring down at me with those big imaginate discs for eyes, and they lit up when he spoke about things he loved. Our eyes finally locked, and I felt like I could look through the prism of his eyes down into his soul if that makes any sense.

"How do they do that?" I questioned.

"Oh, it's not easy," he said. "In fact, it's something most people can't do because they're not open to the idea of it in the first place. Do you understand?"

I nodded yes—but I didn't understand exactly what he meant. I was just really excited to be spending time with him and loved anything he loved. My father had always been such an inquisitive, intelligent person. He knew a lot about a lot of different things. The world had opened up to him in ways most of us will never fully comprehend. And he accepted it all for the taking. He was not going to be restricted in how he looked at things. Of course, I was like a sponge myself, trying to soak it all up. I hung on every word.

"You think I can do that someday?"

"Well, it's definitely possible," he replied. "It just takes some training, but I happen to know that it can be done if you put your mind to it, son. So, here. I want you to lay your head back, close your eyes, and try to remain as calm as possible."

This was fantastic! And I did exactly what he told me to do! Step by step.

He continued.

"I am going to write something down," he said, grabbing a pad and paper. "I am not going to tell you anything about what I write down, and your job is to try and guess what it is I wrote," he added.

After scribbling something down on the piece of paper he folded it up and placed it under his arm for safekeeping.

"Now, start taking in a series of long, deep breaths and clear your mind," he said.

My eyelids were scrunched up tightly as I focused on his voice.

"There ya go," he said. "Deep breaths. Blank Mind. If you sense things here physically call them out, and we will restart."

I was breathing in and out slowly. Moments later, my skin began to tingle, and there was a warmth growing inside of me that I cannot quite describe.

He took me through this whole protracted process, and soon out of the darkness I started to see something. It was mesmerizing.

I guess he could sense the excitement in me growing.

"Now, go to that place," he said calmly, referring to the note he made.

I could see my grandparent's house. It was almost like when I drowned, so the physical barriers meant absolutely nothing. I could move through the door and into their home with ease. Instinctively, I knew they were on their screen porch behind the house, so I moved closer toward them.

I was unsure of what was happening, but I loved it nonetheless and didn't want it to end. Finally, my mind was free to explore. I felt more alive than I'd ever felt before.

However, slowly, I started allowing the doubt to creep back in.

"Stay focused." he repeated.

I didn't know if I was pretending, and this was all made-up in my mind—or if it was real.

He must have sensed my confusion but kept prodding me.

"What do you see?"

"Well," I replied and tried to describe everything I could see. I noted that Grandma and Grandpa were sitting on the porch in their swing. I also saw some other people.

"Good! Now, focus on the other people. What are they doing?" he asked.

"Their mouths are moving. I think they're talking. Hey," I almost shouted. "There's a little boy there, too."

"There is? What is he doing?" Dad asked.

"He's sitting in a little pedal car."

"Are you sure?"

"Yes. I'm sure."

"Tell me about the car. What color is it?"

"It's purple and white. It has fins and a red bow tied around the steering wheel."

"Cline!" Mom shouted, and I snapped back awake. She had walked into the room and was noticeably agitated. "What are you doing with him?" she shouted.

My eyes were now wide open and shifting back and forth between Mom and Dad. I got the impression she had been listening for a while—and was completely disgusted.

Ordinarily, she wouldn't question Dad like that—but this was obviously different. Everything we were doing flew in the face of her beliefs.

"Would you knock it off?" Dad snapped. "I was in the middle of something!"

There was a cigarette hanging from her lips, and she ran over to Dad and reached for me, snatching me up from his lap.

She looked at me worriedly.

"David?"

"Yes, ma'am?"

"Go find the other kids and play with them."

I shook my head and then pulled loose from her grip, as Dad grabbed my other arm in an attempt to hold me there.

He looked directly at me and said, "If you practice that, you'll get better and better at it, okay?"

I shook my head.

"We'll do it again sometime," he added as he slipped the folded piece of paper in my hand and then releasing my arm.

"Go! Go play!" Mom yelled giving me an extra push as I bolted from the room.

At the time, I didn't understand exactly what had happened and why it was such a big issue for my mother.

I ran halfway down to the hall and paused to open the paper. On it, in his handwriting it read "Grandma & Grandpa's House" along with their address and what I would come to learn were the coordinates of where they lived.

However, the truly amazing thing, didn't happen until weeks later when my grandparents arrived. To our surprise, they had the exact same purple and white pedal car that I had viewed in my "dream." It even had the red bow tied firmly attached to the steering wheel.

Once the excitement settled down, I remember asking my grandmother about the car.

She informed me it was for Matt and me. I was thrilled!

"If it's mine, why was a little boy riding it?" I asked her.

She looked at me with a puzzled expression and then walked away.

It was not until a later discussion that I learned they had visitors, and the people had a grandson who was about my age. They had been keeping the little pedal car as a surprise for us stored away on the back porch until they came to see us that day.

However, they did allow the little boy to play with the car when they were visiting to keep him entertained. In other words, the entire image I saw while "dreaming" with Dad was exactly the way things happened, and yet I had no knowledge of it beforehand.

How did dad do that?

In the military world they call this remote viewing, which is something my father was likely involved in first-hand. Of course, we didn't know it at the time. There's a lot of things we didn't know about Dad until years later.

At the time, I was having trouble getting my head around what had happened. As you can imagine, it was all quite confusing.

I assumed at first that I just had a very vivid imagination and made the whole thing up. And yet, once I learned that all of the details were actually true (the exact same as my dream), I didn't know what to make of it.

I didn't even know if what happened was actually a dream or something else. But I don't think I was sleeping. I was awake and following his directions. So, there were more questions than answers then as there is now. That's a theme that keeps running through my life up until this day.

I have lots of questions.

There's never enough answers for me, which is probably why I became a paranormal investigator. I wanted answers.

Now, Dad did do these things we called "party tricks," which is the phrase we used to explain what he did -sometimes when people were over.

Some of the "tricks" were very physical, and others not as much. Mom would tell us that the non-physical ones were "magic tricks." So, in her mind, he was nothing more than a magician with cheap tricks, I suppose.

It was not unusual for my father to do these party tricks when we had people over. Not all of them were "magic," some were just physical. One of his most popular ones was where he would rip through a 7-inch phone book starting with the binding first using his bare hands. And he made it look so simple and effortless.

When I was a kid, these "party tricks" were incredibly impressive. Honestly, I'd have to say they're still pretty impressive. Not everyone found them as impressive as I did, and I was about to find out how un-impressed some people were with my father and his fancy tricks.

CHAPTER 6
The Art of Telling The Truth As A Lie

Despite my reluctance to talk, nonetheless, I started kindergarten. But by that time my fear of saying something wrong was already well ingrained in my psyche. I would struggle to reply to anyone of authority when they talked to me. In fact, it's something I struggled with for all of my years in school. And, If I were being extremely open and honest, I still question opening my mouth at all today from time-to-time.

One day not long after starting school, I was sent to the principal's office for lying. Mother was called in.

My skin was tingling as I sat in the chair waiting for her to arrive. I thought about what I would say and how I should say it, all the while my heart rate was racing in anticipation of what was to come. Of course, me being the hardheaded five-year-old that I was, I was dead set on standing my ground.

I was going to insist on my innocence; after all, I was not lying.

"Today we were sharing stories about our families." the teacher informed my mother as she stood behind the principal's desk with him.

Then he stopped her as if allowing the drama of the day's events to build up. His tactics worked like a charm because I was pretty sure I was going to throw up.

"David," he said, pausing again. "Why don't you just tell your mother what happened. But don't leave out any details," he said, peering down at me from behind his large desk.

I looked at Mom who returned my stares with a painful grimace that suggested she wanted to physically kill me at that very moment.

So, I swallowed hard, mustered my courage, and began.

"I told some people that Dad reads books," I said matter-of-factly.

The anticipation was continuing to mount.

I knew things were about to erupt as my body tensed up in anticipation of what was about to happen.

" And?" he said.

I was slightly confused apparently.

"What else did you say?" he continued.

"Well, I also said that he doesn't use his hands," I muttered.

He slapped his hand down on the desk, and I almost jumped out of my chair.

That's it? I wondered. *Me talking about my father's tricks? It was this big of a deal?*

"I'm confused," Mom admitted.

"So, what your son is saying is that your husband turns the pages of his books without actually touching them, which we all know is impossible," he said. "Unless," he added. "There's something going on in your house that you may want to explain Mrs. Kiefer? It sounds like witchcraft to me," he added and chuckled.

Mom wasn't amused.

I'm still unsure if he actually believed it was witchcraft, or if he was just being coy and trying to press the point that he thought I was lying. One thing was clear, he never once entertained the idea that I was actually telling the truth. His mind went straight to LIE.

"In addition," he added. "Once he was caught in this very obvious lie, he insisted it was all true. In fact, he insisted on this lie being true so much so that he began yelling and acting out in class. He caused so much of a stir that I had to pull him out of his class, which is why I called you today, Mrs Kiefer. I was hoping there was something you could elaborate for me."

Silence followed for what felt like an eternity. My palms were sweating, and I don't think my mother was handling the situation any better.

She stammered and stuttered to come up with a reasonable explanation that would make some amount of sense, and I sat there struggling with what I had said and why it was such a big deal.

To make the finer point, Dad used to read to us sometimes from our kitchen table. And he had this unique talent—if you will. He could turn the pages without touching them. It was something I could not do myself yet. I saw my brothers and sisters attempt it and do it, too. Paul was actually starting to get pretty good at it, but he was nothing like Dad yet.

Mom would catch us practicing, and deep down, I don't think she liked it at all. But it never caused a stir like this at home. For the life of me, I just couldn't figure out what the big deal was.

I still don't. It was positively silly that it was being propelled to this level—and yet, there I was. And there was Mom trying to figure out how to respond to this man who was very emphatic that what had happened was horrible.

"Well," she finally managed to say. "He is obviously lying! You know, to be honest, he often acts out when he is caught in one of his lies, which, as you can imagine, makes things ten times worse," she added.

The principal nodded in agreement.

I could not believe what she was saying.

A lie? I questioned to myself. *What is going on?* I wondered. I knew that I was telling the truth, and the bad thing was, so did she.

I was sitting there trying to bite my tongue—but to be honest, it was getting really hard by the second.

"It's not a lie!" I interjected uncomfortably while squirming in my seat.

"Be quiet young man," the principal replied, pointing his finger at me from behind his desk.

I tried to utter a few more words in my own defense—but it was obviously useless.

My principal and my mother were effectively teaming up on me, at least in my mind. They were both convinced I was a liar, something that shook me to my core. In fact, it has haunted me ever since.

The rest of their conversation was a bit of a blur, and I struggle with relaying exactly what was said. I knew I was telling the truth—but it was pointless to continue to argue.

I don't know if you can relate, but when adults make up their minds, they're made up. That's that.

So, before I knew it, I had been ushered to the corner and asked to bend over and receive my punishment. Back in my younger days, those were called "licks," and when you got in trouble at school that's what you received.

I don't know if he hit me three or four times. I just know how bad it hurt physically. But, to be honest, the emotional toll far outweighed the physical one. Sure. My backside was throbbing once again, but I was shattered from the inside-out. After the first lick, I was already pretty numb to the others anyway.

Worse than anything, my heart was broken.

And as we walked out of the principal's office that day, my mother insisted to the principal that she was sorry for my behavior and that my "licks" would not be the limit to my punishment.

"We're going to continue to address this situation once we go home, sir," she relayed. "I'm terribly sorry for his behavior, and it's inexcusable."

"I appreciate your attention to this," he said, propping the door open. I kept my head down as if to shrink down in size and not be seen, and hopefully, disappear out of existence altogether. That would have suited me just fine to be honest.

The next thing I knew Mom had a firm grip on my forearm and was dragging me down the hall toward the exit.

I had again been labeled a liar, and the label would hang over me for years.

What's probably worse, the kids at school even recognized the fact I had been deemed a liar, and they would often taunt me about it whenever possible.

All the way home Mom scolded me and promised I would have extra chores and all this other stuff—but the damage was already done. At that point, it was adding insult to injury as the adage goes.

I think that's appropriate. If you've ever seen an abused dog (I'm not saying per se that I was abused at that point), but it will have this look of defeat. You can continue to rain the blows down on the dog at that point, but you've already broken its spirits, which is apparently the point.

The whole situation left me wondering if maybe I was a liar. In my mind there was this whole truth thing, and it was apparently alluding me.

So, me being a liar took a firm hold over my life, and I couldn't shake it. Once it started going that direction, it just spiraled out of control.

As an aside, I often tell the story of how I saw an accident in front of our house one day, and I ran back inside to tell everyone about it, but to my dismay, no one believed me. I had burst through the doors, screaming, and carrying on.

In hindsight, the mere fact I had raised my voice at all should've been indication I was telling the truth and that something was wrong. But it was not. I was not to be believed.

That hurts.

It wasn't until the sirens of emergency vehicles came blaring along and everyone saw with their own eyes what happened that they believed me. They had no choice. In any case, the whole way I got branded as "the Liar" is big piece of my paranormal puzzle.

The incident at school continued to bother me all week, but I knew something was up because Mom never told Dad about it. This was a fact I knew because I never got in trouble with him, which was unheard of.

As usual, we never discussed it. It was another thing that seemed to not happen. The whole situation did not sit well with me, even at that age. So, when I had the chance, I took advantage of it.

Saturday, while Dad was sitting in his chair, I slowly approached him quizzically.

"Dad?" I questioned him.

He looked up through his wire-rim glasses.

"Hey little guy," he said, folding the book. "What are you up to?" he added, pulling me up and onto his lap. I stared up at his big eyes looking back at me. I hesitated for a moment, then I asked.

"How can someone tell a lie when they're really telling the truth?" I asked.

Dad just stared back at me puzzled not saying a word. Then, after much thought he asked, "What do you mean?"

Again, I hesitated, then there was movement at the bay window and then a knock at the door.

"I got it Cline," my mother yelled as she entered from the kitchen. As she went to the door Dad slid me off his lap and stood up. We lived in the country. Someone knocking on your door was either a salesman, a Jehovah's Witness, or someone who broke down and needed your help.

"I got it Cel!" Dad ordered, and Mom backed away.

I followed Dad to the door and when he opened it, I saw two men in suits.

"Oh," Dad said surprised, which was odd. Dad was never surprised.

He immediately moved closer to the door and closed it – sticking his head out and holding the door tightly so no one could see or hear what was being said.

I still remember how odd that was. I had never seen Dad do that. They mumbled a bit and being small, I tried to squeeze between Dad and the door to see more. Dad immediately pushed me back. Within seconds, he shut the door and looked at Mom.

"I got to go!" he said staring right at her.

"What?" my mother replied in disbelief.

"It's work," he said, opening his eyes wide.

"You just got here Cline," she shot back and followed him back to their bedroom. Within minutes, Dad came up the hall with his suitcase in tote. Mom came after him a buzz of questions.

"Why did they come for you?" she asked.

"We have no phone. How else were they going to get ahold of me?" he shot back.

"Well, how am I supposed to do what we planned?"

She stopped.

Dad was staring at her sternly.

"Look, I have to go!" he insisted.

I immediately ran to the large bay window and watched as the two black cars quickly backed down the driveway with my father following closely behind.

"Well isn't that just a crock?" Mom said taking a puff off her cigarette.

I turned to her and asked, "Who are those people?"

She sat on the couch and patted the seat cushion beside her, suggesting I take a seat.

"That's your Daddy's work. He is really important. He is only one of a few people in the world who can do his job."

"Oh," I replied. And just as calmly and tenderly as she said it, she changed her mood and added, "And it's just a crock that they do that to him and ruin our whole weekend!"

Dad was gone and so was my chance to finally unlock this truth thing I had been wondering about. Our weekend and time with him was also gone. We spent the rest of the time beside ourselves without him. I didn't know what Dad did for a living at that point, but it seemed pretty important for them to come all the way out there and get him like that.

CHAPTER 7
Ready or Not, Here I Come

Things were changing all the time and not only with me but with my whole family—and between my parents. The day that fact became obvious was a dark one, and I'll never forget what happened.

Was it paranormal related? I cannot tell you. Did something become entangled with our family? I cannot tell you. What I can say is that the spiritual world seemed to be opening up to me. My first undeniable dark experience was during a game with my siblings.

It was after dinner and dark. Mom and Dad sat downstairs in front of the large fireplace. Us kids sat on the concrete near them. The fireplace was often the place Dad would gather us and tell stories or talk history. Tonight, was a quiet night. We all watched the flames dance in silence.

"I'm bored!" Paul said. Mary and Susan replied with a "me too". "Let's go up and play a game." Mary suggested. Quickly they were up and heading to the stairs.

"Me too!" I said and began to follow.

Susan quickly turned to add "Just the older kids. You're too young."

"Dad!" I exclaimed.

"Include the other kids." He ordered.

"But we don't know what we are going to play." Paul added. "Wait til we see what we are going to play." He said staring at me. For me it was a solid way to get out of involving me. Later, I would wish they hadn't included me.

The older kids trekked their way up the stairs and I returned back to Mom and Dad.

"Come here." Dad said as I returned reaching out his hands to me. Excited, I rushed to him. He plopped me on his lap. There was silence and just the occasional pop from the wood as it burned. I loved time on Dad's lap. Having his attention. And I think he enjoyed it just as much. Afterall, the other kids were getting older and were less lap kids than myself and Matt.

"I'm going up to get another drink and use the bathroom." Mom said a short time later.

"Grab me a pack." Dad replied needing more cigarettes.

Mom was barely at the stairs when Dad said to me "See the flames?"

"Yeah." I eagerly replied. What was he up to? What story or lesson did he have ready to tell?

"Pay attention to how they move." He said. I watched the flames dance in the fireplace. Then, Dad added "See if you can move the flames like this." I watched a bluish orange and yellow flame extend itself higher than the others and dance- swaying back and forth.

I began to concentrate on one flame. A small one as even as the others. "Concentrate" Dad said. I tried, but to no avail. "Come on. You can do it. Really concentrate.". I tried again but to no avail again. Then Dad said. "Follow me and do what I do." I watched as one of the flames started to glow and dance higher than the others. "Come on. Try." He insisted.

Again, I tried, but again nothing. "I am no good."

"It just takes practice like anything else." Dad replied. "Watch this" he said. I watched intently as he brought two separate flames higher and higher. They would dance and move closer changing colors with their length.

I began to laugh at watching them dance.

"What is so funny?"

In the concentration of watching my father's entertaining trick and laughing we must have not heard Mom return.

"Nothing" Dad replied as the two dancing flames he once controlled fell back in line with the others.

"Did you remember my pack? Dad asked holding his empty one up.

"You're out!" Mom answered.

"Well, looks like it is time for a trip to town." Dad slid me off his lap and got up from his lawn chair. "Let's go." he said looking at Mom.

"Can I go, Dad?" I eagerly asked.

"No, you should go play with the other kids." Mom quickly replied.

I understood that having five kids and Dad being gone all week gave them little time together, but I still wanted time with Dad too.

We trekked up the stairs to the kitchen in darkness. The older kids must have been in one of their rooms playing.

"Kids!" Dad's booming voice rang out. "We're going to town."

The older kids made their way to the kitchen with their own questions.

Mom assured them too that they must stay and then added "And keep an eye on your brother." Then, "We are taking Matt with us.". Matt, since he was so young, was always allowed to go with them.

I watched as Mom scooped up Matt hoping they would change their mind, but as quickly as they decided they were out the door and gone. I watched from the bay window as they rolled down the driveway and down the street. I hoped still that they would change their mind. They didn't.

"What are we gonna do now?" Susan asked.

"Let's play flashlight hide and go seek." Mary exclaimed.

Growing up, there were times when we did not have electricity, so we had to get creative to keep ourselves entertained. This is how the game was born. The rules were the same as Hide and Seek, only in the dark and with a flashlight.

I was getting older, and it was my turn to be "it" by myself. I loved flashlight hide-and-seek except those times when I was alone in the darkness.

"One, two, three, four, five, six, seven, eight, nine, and ten!" I screamed, denoting I was ready to start making my way through the house.

"Ready or not here I come!" I shouted as I eased forward in the darkness.

The whole house was dark and quiet. My siblings were hiding in various places. I took my flashlight and scanned the kitchen first. Up and down and side to side the light beam danced across the family kitchen and dining area but no one was in sight. I looked under the table. I opened up a couple of cabinet doors with the enthusiasm of someone who just knew they were about to bust someone hiding. But no one was here.

After a couple of minutes, I was content that no one was hiding in the kitchen, so I made my way toward the living room.

I saw the old, dusty bookshelf, the recliner, and other furniture. I looked around the back of things, under things, around things. Nothing.

No one was in there, which told me they had to be in the bedrooms. They weren't in the kitchen or living room. I was slowly eliminating rooms one by one.

However, as I got to our long, dark hallway I paused.

To be perfectly clear, I hated that damn hall. It was so long that it represented a million opportunities for one of them to jump out and scare the crap out of me—and they usually did. In fact, that usually resulted in me quitting and ending the whole game right there on the spot.

As I shined the flashlight down the hall, I saw something. Someone peeked their head out from Mom and Dad's door frame. That was halfway down the hall. I bravely told myself "I can make it."

I stepped forward gently. The boards under my feet cracked and echoed as I placed my weight on them.

I took another step and then another step.

"I see you," I said, grinning. "You're down there aren't you?"

I didn't know who I was talking to but clearly someone was down there. And I knew that I only needed to find the first one so that I would not be alone anymore.

So, I continued to creep my way down the hall toward my parent's room, figuring someone was down at the end somewhere. They had just revealed their head and then snatched it back—or so it appeared. How obvious could you make it?

As I got closer down the hall, I could hear the giggling. It was one of the girls.

I finally got to Mom and Dad's room doorway as the giggling got just a little bit louder. I was growing in confidence by the second.

I shined my light toward the walk-in closet where the giggles were coming from.

"Ready or not here I come," I repeated coyly.

This is going to be easy, I thought to myself.

I creeped closer to the door and then reached my tiny hand out to grab the knob. I jerked the door back.

"Gotcha!" I exclaimed.

Wait, I thought. No one's in here.

I shined my light into the closet under the clothes and around them. Nothing.

Not possible, I thought.

"Come on! I got ya! Come out!" I cried. "I heard ya giggling. Get outta there!"

No one revealed themselves, so I began poking around behind the hanging clothes and shining my light. Still nothing. It didn't make any sense. I knew I had heard something coming from this closet.

I heard the giggles again—but this time they were coming from outside their closet somewhere.

I left the closet determined to find them more now.

As I got closer, the giggles got louder.

I could hear the cabinet under the bathroom sink slam shut.

They must have really thought they fooled me, I thought.

I was almost angry that I fell for it, but I wasn't going to let them scare me anymore. And, I knew I finally had them cornered now.

So, I entered the bathroom in Mom and Dad's room.

I ran to the cabinet door and whipped it open.

"Caught you!" I exclaimed proudly but nothing, except some miscellaneous toiletries stared back at me.

They had somehow managed to trick me again.

I stood back up, scratching my head, realizing there was only one other place that they could possibly be hiding.

I looked over at the shower curtain with my flashlight.

It was perfectly still, but I just knew someone was behind it. They must have slammed the cabinet door as they ran by and hid behind the shower curtain to throw me off. Judging by the girlish giggles, I had a pretty good idea who that would be.

I walked over to the shower and grabbed the curtain.

"I got you now!" I yelled and pulled the curtain back with great enthusiasm.

Nothing but an empty tub and shower.

"Hey, where are you guys at?" I asked to no one in particular and wheeled around in the dark bathroom. I was starting to get scared.

I turned toward the doorway and shined my light toward the hall and noticed Paul standing there looking back as if they had no clue what I was doing.

"What the heck are you doing in here?" he asked.

"The girls were in here hiding," I replied. "I heard them. But they somehow got away," I added.

"You know we are not allowed to hide in their room. They're not in here. Come on. Let's go. We're gonna get in trouble."

"But one of the girls was in here," I pled with him. It wasn't fair! They could hide in here, but I couldn't go get them?

"David, the girls are right here," he replied, shinning his flashlight behind him.

Susan was standing behind him looking at me more confused.

Wait. What? I wondered. Did they sneak out of the bathroom when I looked under the sink? I thought. I knew I should have checked under the bed, I figured.

"We weren't in there!" she exclaimed. "And you shouldn't be either!"

She looked at Mary and said, "He doesn't know how to play this game. He's the worst finder ever. Come on. Let's go," she added, and they walked back up the hall.

The little hairs on my arm were standing up again. Something was in there. I knew it. I thought it was my sister or sisters but if not them, who? I wondered.

Paul grabbed my hand and jerked me out of their room and up the hall toward the Living Room.

"You're hurting my arm!" I snapped.

"A lot more than that's gonna be hurting if you go back in their room," he warned.

Once we got there, Paul explained the terms.

"Look, we're going to do this again. David, you're still it, so count to ten again. We're going to hide again but NOT in Mom and Dad's room. You can try again to find us. We'll make it easy. You only need to get one of us, deal?"

"I don't know," I replied, still confused as to what happened earlier.

"Come on, David," Mary said. "It's not that hard. You can do it. We'll hide. Just make sure not to go in Mom and Dad's room again. We'll make it super easy this time. Ready?"

I shook my head okay, albeit hesitantly. Paul was the boss. He was the oldest. He was our leader. We all looked up to him, and he knew it.

I began to count.

Their movements slowly faded as they disappeared somewhere in the back of the house.

"One, two, three," I counted. I kept going until I finally reached ten. "Ready or not here I come!" I yelled and turned to the big dark room.

I had to find them this time. I had to prove Susan wrong. Even if it took a little more time or effort, I was determined that I was going to find them this time.

I realized pretty quickly that they weren't hiding in the living room. That would have been way too easy, I guess. So, I repeated my steps from last time and wanted to check off the kitchen, although I halfway assumed, they weren't there either.

As I crossed from the Livingroom to get to the Kitchen, I passed the end of the hall as a knot formed in my throat. As noted, I hated that long, dark hallway.

I flashed my light all the way down the hall, where we had a pantry at the furthest end.

There were several large shelves and a big wicker basket for dirty clothes at the bottom. My parents called it the "hamper," and it was the perfect size to hide in.

My light caught the lid just right, and I could see it cracked open. Paul's words went through my head again.

"We're going to make it easy for you," he said a few minutes earlier, and sure enough, I could see him. Just half his face, his cheek pressed against the lid, but Paul was in the clothes hamper peeking out at me probably with a huge grin on his face.

My heart was elated. I had found someone.

"I found you!" I yelled. He really had made it easy on me, perhaps too easy, I thought. "You can come out now. I see you!" I added, thinking he would just give up.

He didn't come out.

Nothing.

He was inside the basket and had now turned his head, and it was sticking up beyond the lid peering back at me. His eyes twinkled in the light of my flashlight.

Apparently, he was going to make me come get him knowing my fear of being alone. Or maybe he was baiting me so that one of the girls could jump out and scare me.

So, I moved forward cautiously. One step, another, then another. I paused with a thought.

If I ran to the hamper, maybe the girls could not get me, I figured. Maybe I could be quick enough, I thought, so I started rushing toward the hamper, quickly closing the space.

As I began to run, he dropped the lid and tucked away inside before I got there.

I knew he was caught and reached for the hamper lid.

"I got you!" I yelled. I pulled the lid back, content that I had just won our game. He was 'it' now, I figured.

But the hamper was about half empty except for some clothes.

I immediately deduced that he was hiding under the clothes and started pulling them out one by one.

Still nothing.

I was throwing shirts out of the closets, socks, miscellaneous other clothes. Finally, I was at the bottom.

No one's in there, I realized, and my heart sank.

I had just seen him!

"What are you doing?" Paul exclaimed. He turned on the light in the hall and was standing behind me.

I looked at him then back at the empty basket. Impossible, I figured.

"How'd you do that?" I quietly asked.

"Do what?" he replied.

Paul and the girls started approaching me.

"We were all hiding together in the kitchen on the other side of the breakfast bar. We thought it was the first place you would look," Paul admitted. "I told you I was going to make it easy. "

I stood there, stunned.

"You better pick up the mess you made before Mom sees it," he cautioned me.

"I'm done!" Mary exclaimed as she walked past me to their room.

"Me too!" Susan angrily added. "You are no good at this. In fact, I think you may be the absolute worst finder in the entire world."

I stood there, trying to gather myself.

What just happened? I wondered.

Did Paul find a way to do one of Dad's party tricks?

I still cannot say for sure what happened. But I do know that since that day I was terrified of the hamper. I'd often see the lid of it flapping open and closed from a distance. After that, it just terrified me.

From then on, I would always ask or ensure that the closet at the end of the hallway was shut. I would also try to dodge being "it" as much as possible. I just didn't like being alone in the dark like that.

Growing up can be really, really hard. That's true for almost every child, and the challenges and difficulties will inevitably vary from person to person.

For me, I was trying to deal with hard issues about life and death and had no one to turn to, not even my father who probably had far more answers about these subjects than anyone else.

The fact I couldn't speak with him freely, led me to questioning his beliefs and abilities for a time. I would often wonder how he didn't notice I was struggling or do anything about it if he did notice. And that bothered me a lot.

I came to find out that he was dealing with more than I knew about at the time, but that came much later in life. And, as quickly as I had doubted my father's beliefs and abilities, he would do something that would make me start to believe all over again.

CHAPTER 8
Darkness Creeps Closer

That whole week seemed to go by slowly, especially since the other kids seemed to still be mad at me for the events during hide and seek. Matt always seemed to have Mom's attention like any three or four-year-old should, but back then, I didn't seem to understand. I was too young for the older kids and too old for Mom's attention. I learned to just start doing stuff alone.

Occasionally, Matt would come in and try and play, but he was younger, and it was hard to really play along with him. Today was one of those days.

From day one, Matt had a system with his cars. He would line them up nose to tail as long as he could and move the first one, then the second one, and down the line. When he got to the end, he would start the process all over again. And if you hit or accidentally moved a car, he would have to start the process all over again, too. I mean, that would really bug him.

I was just the opposite. I was crashing cars, making my cars jump, rollover, and race.

When Matt wanted a car, he would just walk over and take it to add to his stream of perfectly aligned cars.

"Mom," I yelled. "He's taking my car!"

"Play nice!" Mom yelled from the kitchen.

A short time later, Matt came and took another one.

"No!" I told him, but he took it anyway.

I rolled off of my belly and onto my back. I gave up on playing and just stared at the ceiling for a while. Then I heard Paul come in.

"Did you take the trash down to burn?" Mom asked.

"I'll do it later," he replied.

"I said to do it now!" Mom snapped back at him. Her tone was off. Mom rarely yelled like that. It grabbed my attention, and I started to get up and head into the kitchen.

"Mom, it's windy, and," Paul tried to explain, but Mom stopped him.

"I said to do it now! Do you get me, young man?" she snapped again.

I stood between the two rooms. Paul was trying to get a drink. Mom was sitting at the table eating.

Paul attempted to get himself some food, and he once again tried to explain, "But Mom with the wind..."

I never saw Mom or anyone else snap. But I believe that is what happened. In an instant, she picked up the lemonade glass and threw it across the room. It missed, but it still left Paul cowering and every bit as shocked as I was.

That's when my sensation began to hit me again. Something was going on. Mom's expression changed. Her voice was a bit deeper and different somehow.

"Now son, you come here right now!" she said, standing at the table with a look as if she was ready to charge.

I was in awe. Paul was still cowering from across the kitchen. He slowly shook his head no.

Mom instantly headed to the tack board where the paddle was hanging. It was missing. She began to search with her eyes and move around the kitchen, looking in various drawers frantically.

The whole scene seemed odd. First, I never heard her call anyone of us boys or girls like that. It was always our name, and if we were in trouble, it was by our first and middle name.

What's odder, this was HER kitchen, she knew right where everything was located (because she put it there). How did she not know where things were now? Why was she searching for things as if she was new to our house?

Then I realized even her mannerisms were not the same as normal. Mom always moved quick, but this seemed to be too quick. And Mom was never panicked or frantic. If something got to her, she would sit and place her head in her hands to calm down.

However, now, all of the sudden, she was doing the opposite, shifting things on the counter, opening drawers to search them like a crazy person. It was really unnerving.

Finally, something grabbed her attention on the counter. My father's hammer. It was still there from the work he had done over the previous weekend. Her eyes locked on that thing like a laser, and she darted and grabbed it before turning her attention back to Paul.

"Come here, boy," she commanded, readying the hammer as if to strike him.

My heart was beating in my chest, and the tingling sensations escalated. *No,* I thought, but I dared not to make a peep.

Paul stood still frozen with his eyes wide open. And again, this time with minimal movement, he shook his head no.

Wham! Mom slammed the hammer against the counter and raised it up again. Paul and I both jumped. Wham! Again. No words, no commands, just wham!

Then, she took a step closer to him. Paul was still frozen in his tracks like a dear in headlights. Wham! And another step almost rhythmically. Wham!

By now, she was only three feet from him. Paul was just standing there perfectly still. I watched as she raised back the hammer to ready the next swing. Paul was now in range.

Without a thought, I gasped.

Instantly, she stopped and turned to me. It was then that I realized the difference. Not only were her mannerisms not her own, but her face seemed different. It was slightly contorted and awkward. And her eyes were dark, completely devoid of any natural color.

At that moment, I briefly flashed to images of the body floating in the pond and realized, this isn't my mother. She was a wrapper for something else and almost pulled it off. But I could see through it, and I was terrified.

Whatever it was, it was staring right back at me.

"You," it said, pointing the hammer at me. "Come here," it ordered.

I looked to Paul for help. He was our fearless leader. But he just stared at me in shock with his eyes wide open.

Did he recognize that this was not Mom, too? Or, was he just as surprised by her actions as me?

I shook my head hesitantly as if to plead with it, "No!"

It reached out and grabbed Paul by the arm and pulled him like a rag doll across the room toward me and the table. Paul was 17 and athletic. He could easily handle my mother's small frame physically if he needed to. It seemed to have twice the strength as my own mother. As they approached the table, the chair pulled itself out, and it plopped Paul down.

He had submitted himself over to its whims without resistance.

By now, it's attention went back to me. It's dark eyes stared a hole straight through me, and then it commanded, "Come here!"

Again, I shook my head no.

Then, in an instant, Mom's voice came back.

"David Christopher! Your brother is in trouble, and you are going to help him learn his punishment."

I got chills, and my sensations got worse. Plus my ears were ringing so loud it was drowning out my thoughts. I hesitantly took a step or two, but suddenly I was there in front of it, and Paul was in the chair.

What had happened? Did I move quick and not realize it?

It moved from behind Paul in the chair and got closer to me.

"Take the hammer," it said in my mother's voice but deeper and more hollow.

It stretched it's arms out with the hammer in tow as if to offer me a token gift. My stomach turned, and I felt like I was going to throw up. Again, I shook my head no.

It drew the hammer back over its shoulder, ready to strike. I jumped in fear.

"Would you prefer I punish him?" it asked, devilishly.

That's when the tears came. I just couldn't take it anymore. My stomach turned over, and I wretched but the vomit wouldn't come.

How I didn't throw up at that exact moment, I never knew. No, I shook my head, and again it offered the hammer up to me like this was some kind of sick, twisted ritual.

At that point, albeit hesitantly, I took the hammer. I stared back at it. Those evil black eyes were devoid of any life or humanity. This was *not* my mother, but I had no idea what it was, what it wanted, or how to deal with it.

"We need to punish him, David," it informed me.

It was almost as if it was taking joy in the whole process.

"Are you ready, David?" it asked.

Did it expect me to answer? Did it want me to say something?

I just wanted the whole thing over. Paul sat dazed in the chair, no struggle, no acknowledgement of what was happening.

"Hit his foot," it said.

I was shocked. So shocked I hesitantly replied, "What?"

It stepped closer to me.

"I said, David Christopher, to hit his foot!"

I didn't know what to do. I was frozen.

The ringing in my ears was replaced with the sounds of this devil's voice echoing through my skull.

"Hit his foot! Hit his foot!" it kept screaming.

By now, I was shaking as the tears ran down my face.

Every time it yelled at me, I cowered just a little bit more in fear. I don't know how I kept from dropping the hammer, but I managed to keep ahold of it while shaking tremendously.

"Hit his foot!" it kept commanding.

I shook my head no and briefly took my eyes off of it and knelt down next to Paul.

From my knees, I looked back up at it, and it was savoring what was happening.

I started crying even harder.

"Do it!" it yelled and simultaneously it seemed like its voice echoed- no physically rattled the whole house.

I looked around the kitchen in fear.

It crept closer toward me like it was about to pounce. I have never felt so utterly defeated and hopeless as I felt in that exact moment.

"Do it!" it commanded

I finally lined up a swing and looked at Paul as if to say, "I'm sorry." I think I was going to hit him. I had no choice.

The whole time, he was just dazed. I mean, there was no reaction whatsoever.

Was this him or was he a wrapper, too? I wondered. *No, that's him. That's my brother!*

I knew that was Paul's foot, and I didn't want to hurt him. It was unconscionable. Paul saved me. I was here breathing because of what he did.

How could I hurt him?

Not to mention, Paul was a tremendous athlete back then. He played football, baseball, and ran track for the school. There was no way I could hit his feet, which were literally his life.

I started thinking really quickly.

I stalled by lining up the hammer once again but pausing. And then it occurred to me. I was kneeled down like I was proposing to someone, and both of our feet were a few inches apart.

So, I drew back the hammer for a third time, deciding I would strike. I brought the hammer down with great force. Wham!

I consciously redirected the hammer hitting my toes. The pain was excruciating, and without thought, I yelled, "Oh, God. Help me!"

I crumbled to the floor and clutched at my foot. As I looked up through the tears, I saw my mother staring down at me in shock.

Paul rushed to me and asked, "What did you do?"

He pulled me off the floor and sat me in the chair.

"You smashed your toes! He needs ice!" he yelled.

A calmness fell across the kitchen, but my foot was on fire.

"Mom! David needs ice!" he repeated.

My mother snapped out of it and ran to grab some ice.

"It doesn't look good," he said, pulling my hands away.

Mom rushed back with ice tucked tightly inside a white dishrag and handed it to Paul.

My toes were throbbing, and as I looked at Mom, her whole expression had changed. She now had this dazed look on her face. But she couldn't make eye contact with me. It's like she was ashamed.

Maybe she couldn't grasp what happened? Maybe she didn't know what was going on; after all, she was just a wrapper for this other thing. I don't know what it was.

Paul eventually carried me to the couch and propped my foot up with ice on it. He spent the rest of the day by my side. Every time the ice started to melt inside the rage, he would hurry into the kitchen, fetch some more from the ice trays in the freezer, and replace them.

When the other kids asked us what happened, Paul just said I was helping him and got hurt. No more details than that.

Did he know? Was he there watching? Or was he gone like I was when I drowned?

As far as Mom, she avoided us altogether for several days- or at least as much as she could. And in the typical family fashion, we somehow knew not to discuss it. In fact, this is the first time this incident has ever been mentioned in decades.

I struggle to write the words, because the whole thing shook me to my core. It was that bad. I had watched my own mother be taken over by some sort of malevolent creature of some sort. She was a wrapper for a demon or evil spirit—or whatever you want to call it.

As the days and weeks passed by after the incident, things started to return to normal. My toes hurt, but not enough to slow me down when I really wanted to do something.

And, as noted, we never discussed the incident with anyone, especially Mom. She never apologized or even acknowledged it happened. But, afterwards, I never once saw my mother in the same light or not, possessed or otherwise. I still harbored some anger for what she did or was a part of.

Was it her fault? I don't know. But that's how I felt. Can you blame me? No matter what, she was still my mom, but she was different. It seemed to change her.

As far as dad goes, I never really knew how to bring it up to him. Dad was busy in those days anyway. In fact, it was right about then that he started to miss certain weekends coming home.

Mom said it was just his work needed him, and he was all tied up with important things that were beyond his control. She would explain, "It was better that we know he is not coming home, then he gets home and has to leave us again anyway. That way, we aren't as disappointed and can plan our weekends better," she would add.

She had her own way of coping with his absence. Now, as far as us kids, we would try and do our chores as if Dad was coming home because you never know. Sometimes he would.

At the same time, the house just wasn't the same without him in it and his constant direction. We would fumble through the chores the best we could to ensure we did our duties as part of the team. Like Dad used to say if just one of the fingers on that big proverbial fist fails, the whole team fails, and we didn't want that either.

I guess you could say we were a pretty tight-knit group even though we never talked about some of the strange experiences around the house.

. . .

DURING ONE AFTERNOON, I found myself grounded again. Apparently, when working in the garden pulling weeds, I was not watching where I stepped and trampled several plants.

It was not my fault.

I was literally being tempted away by the prairie girl and her mischievous brother. Every time I would look up or wipe the sweat from my brow, they would wave or stare at me, and I just had to wave back or smile.

I wanted to get the work done so I could maybe sneak off or play with them. But in my eagerness to finish, I ended up getting grounded.

Later that evening, in my usual stubbornness, I ended up being the last one at the dinner table. Yet again, I had been punished for my lies, and I sat at the table eating alone.

I refused to eat the plate that sat in front of me. It was liver and onions, which is gross just thinking about now. In addition, I knew once I was done, it was back to chores, reading the bible, or my going to my room (under punishment, you were not allowed to play games with the other kids).

My mother was insistent.

"You finish, or you are not going to leave this table."

She paused for a moment and stared at me, contemplating my irrational stubbornness.

"Dishes are washed, so you wash your own plate when you are done," she ordered.

The she left to go to see what the other kids were up to.

It wasn't long when I heard the kids playing tag in the basement. I stayed there quietly for a while, but the activities were too much for me to take. So, I slowly got up from my chair and made it to the top of the stairs. The kids were playing down there, but the lights appeared to be off, which was odd.

Then, in a flash, I saw a girl's dress as she ran by the doorway. The funny thing was it was not one of my sister's dresses. It looked more like the prairie girl's dress from the field.

It never occurred to me to be scared. It never occurred to me to be "freaked out." Heck, I was excited.

I had always wanted to play with her and her brother, and apparently, they were here now to do just that. So, I rushed down to the bottom of the stairs, calling out to her the whole time.

"Hello!" I yelled. "I am here! I am here! Let's play together!"

Out of the still darkness of the basement, I heard the faint sound of little kids' giggles. Then, I heard them running away.

Though I was afraid of the dark, in desperation, I decided to follow suit.

'Hey, wait up!" I yelled. "I'll even be it," I tried to explain.

I finally stopped, deciding to count, and turned to the door.

"One, two, three, four," I counted. As I made my way to ten, my heart got louder and louder in my chest. Everything was drowned out by my beating heart. Yet, the basement was silent.

When I reached ten, I turned and stared into the darkness.

"Ready or not here I come."

I took a few hesitant steps deeper into the darkness and away from the light of the upstairs.

Nothing.

Silence.

A laugh then materialized from the other side of the basement, and I beelined toward the sound as quickly as I could with my arms outstretched to feel through the darkness.

As I entered the other side (that side had windows), the light from outside shown in just enough to see two silhouettes. I relaxed my arms a bit in front of me, but lower.

"I hear you," I said, and heard another giggle.

I noticed something in the far corner. I inched my way closer. It appeared to be the little boy who was standing to the side in the shadow of Dad's workbench.

"I see you! You're gonna be it," I said in excitement. Finally, finally, I had some friends to play with, I assumed.

Just then, a big whoosh blew by me in the darkness. The little girl ran right in front of my face between her brother and me while giggling.

She's not good at this, I thought, but I was still having fun.

After she ran past, I immediately took off in pursuit. I cannot believe how fast she was. She managed to run two full circles around the large basement, and I could not for the life of me seem to catch her.

As she ran, she laughed. And pretty soon, I joined in with her. We laughed together as we ran, but I couldn't close the gap between us no matter how hard I tried.

Finally, she darted over to the far side of the basement and paused. This was my shot, I figured. I was going to get her this time.

I pursued her quickly, and as I approached her, I slowed down because it was getting darker and darker where she was at.

In fact, she had disappeared entirely.

"Hey, I know you're in here," I said as I passed in front of the stairs. Then, something grabbed my hand, and I immediately started to panic. It was pulling me.

"What's going on? Stop!" I cried.

It was starting to hurt.

"David Christopher!" she yelled. I had never heard her say anything other than laugh, but her voice was mean and hateful now.

I struggled to pull away from her, but she had the strength of two adult men. It was utterly useless.

"Stop it! You're hurting me!" I cried.

She just kept pulling me closer and closer toward the stairs and into the light.

What the heck is happening? I wondered.

Finally, we reached the bottom step, and I looked up. Mom had a hold of my arm and was pulling me up the steps.

Somehow the fun and excitement of playing with my friends, my mother had entered the basement and was pulling me back upstairs and into the kitchen where she felt like I belonged.

I was further grounded and took the punishment silently. Of course, I didn't open my mouth or mention it to anyone. Who would have believed me?

CHAPTER 9
An Enemy at Our Door

"David, wake up," Paul said quietly. He was shaking me furiously.

"What?" I said, trying to wake up. I didn't know what time it was, but it was in the middle of the night, and I had been in a dead sleep.

"Get up!" Paul said. "Dad wants us."

At the same time, Mom grabbed Matt from his bed in our room, and we slowly made our way into the kitchen. The whole thing felt like big dream that we were somehow experiencing simultaneously.

The house was pitch black, so Paul led me by the hand. My eyes were finally starting to get adjusted when I noticed everyone else standing around in the kitchen, and the girls were visibly upset.

Dad sat quietly at the end of the table staring out the patio door into the backyard or just beyond in the woods. So, finally, we all huddled behind him, trying to figure out what all the excitement was about.

"What's going on?" I asked.

"Shuuuussshh!" Paul snapped.

We stood in a huddled silence, while Dad concentrating on whatever was happening in the backyard.

"There, do you see them?" he said to no one in particular.

I looked at Mom and noticed disbelief in her face. Mary was quietly weeping. Susan held her doll and was looking at it. Matt was in Mom's arms and Paul—the always dutiful son—was reporting back like some soldier, while standing attentively by Dad's side. I didn't know what was going on, but this definitely was not a normal occurrence – not even for our *para*-normal family.

"No, Cline I don't," she said.

"Look, back by the tree line. You don't see that movement?"

"No, I just don't see anything."

Dad was seeing something. She wasn't seeing it. No one else was either. It was the strangest thing. He had gathered us in the dark of night and was concerned about something in the backyard, but I had no idea what it was. Maybe the old man had finally lost his marbles altogether, I wondered.

But we dared not question him, so we just sat there silently, looking.

"I'm going back to bed," Susan said starting to move toward the hallway.

Dad, without breaking his stare pushed his arm out behind himself to stop her.

"I said, we need to stay here," he said with a concern in his voice I hadn't noticed until now.

Mom cautiously drew her back into the huddle like a protective momma bear guarding her young.

"Kids, you see them, right?" Dad whispered.

I didn't see anything, but I wanted to. So, we all began to concentrate out the backyard harder than ever. I stared into the darkness, but there was nothing there.

"Look with your *inner* self," Dad added.

When he would say this, it was because he wanted us to look not only with our physical eyes but with our spiritual. He had taught us from a very young age that we are physical beings with physical sight but that we are also spiritual beings with spiritual sight and can see beyond the physical plane.

I tried to play along. So, as Dad advised, I opened myself up just like he taught us. Once I did that, I looked back outside again. Of course, there was nothing but darkness, but I continued to concentrate all my senses on whatever it was he was seeing.

And there it was.

Finally, I noticed small movements in the backyard like silhouettes amidst the tree line. I also started sensing something.

I'm not a gifted author and have struggled putting my experiences down on paper, but what I saw could only be described as some sort of spiritual creatures, which were moving around by the tree line.

Lurking.

Slithering near the ground.

Others were floating just above the ground.

Some of them were completely devoid of any definable shape.

I wondered how I could see darkness in the darkness. They were black against a back drop of darkness, so they were really hard to spot at first—but once you did, there was no mistaking it. They were there. And I was even starting to define them better, too.

It is as if they were a different shade of blackness, an indescribable, almost unearthly hue of black. But they gave off a dim light (but not real light as we know it). It was not enough to be bright or light up.

"Do you see them?" he repeated.

A couple of us told him that we did. And for a moment, I wondered if this was one of Dad's party tricks.

How was he doing this? I wondered.

"It is a spiritual attack," he replied quietly, sternly.

His words brought the fear back. I started losing my concentration all over again. I don't know if Dad sensed it or just happened to say the next words.

"Just concentrate. Don't let them scare you. They are nothing, nothing! Just some low-level bullshit bullies."

"Oh, Cline. Come on, kids. Let's all go back to bed," she said.

It was then that I realized Mom really could not see them like some of us. They were there, they could be seen if she would try. Paul and I saw them. But not her. It's like she was immune to sensing what was happening on a spiritual level.

Dad hit the table with his fist, and Mom stopped in her tracks.

"I said, stay here! I am trying to protect us!"

I watched these things go back and forth amongst the tree line.

Were they watching us watch them?

Then it became apparent there were more of them. And they were in the field, as well.

"Dad?" I asked, worriedly.

"I know. They are gathering around us in formation."

"It's like an attack," Paul said.

"It *is* an attack," Dad admitted.

They were getting closer and closer to the house.

"BANG! BANG! BANG!"

We all jumped and turned toward the front doors. Dad maintained his concentration and didn't react. Did he sense it before it happened? Could he tell or sense them without seeing them?

I looked at my mother and for once saw true terror in her eyes. In fact, it was the first time, I think, I ever saw fear in her face.

"BANG! BANG! BANG!"

My father clinched his fists tightly as if he was readying himself to fight a playground bully.

The front doors started to rattle. I don't know how they kept from flying off the hinges.

Needless to say, all hell broke loose (pardon the pun).

The entire house started shaking on its foundation. The lights were flickering on and off. The cabinets in the kitchen started banging open and shut.

Some glassware spilled to the floor and shattered.

The spiritual beings in the yard began to move swiftly and chaotically around the backyard like an angry pack of hyenas. The kitchen table started to rumble and the floor below my feet was starting to shift. I almost lost my balance, which broke my concentration momentarily; however, at this point, there was no mistaking what I saw.

The whole family huddled together with the girls starting to cry. I would have too, but I was too afraid to make a noise.

Everything Dad had ever said was coming to fruition. If ever there had been the tiniest seed of doubt in my mind, it was completely gone now.

We were under attack from some sort of malevolent spiritual beings that were clearly not there to be our friends. These were the evil kind and were doing everything in their power to let us know they were there—with us—to do us harm.

I noticed that Dad was completely silent at that point.

I don't know how long it all lasted. In hindsight, I think it only lasted 20 to 30 seconds, but it was pure mayhem and felt like it lasted much longer.

Finally, as quickly as it began, it stopped.

Dead silence.

The girls had even stopped crying and were looking around as if to expect the next item in the cabinets to fall.

Matt wasn't even crying anymore.

Mom was trying to console and comfort the girls and my baby brother.

Dad was breathing deeper and quicker than before. For the first time, he moved a little bit then looked down at the table.

Sweat was falling from his brow in sheets.

"Cline?" Mom asked, breaking the silence. "What the hell was that?"

Yeah, Dad! What was that? I thought. Even Mom had recognized that something had happened. I mean, there was absolutely no denying it at this point.

All Dad had said was that they were just some kind of "low-level bullshit bullies." That was low-level?

What just happened? I wondered.

For what felt like the longest time, he wouldn't respond as if he was still coming to grips with what happened (or still rattled).

But, to his credit, he was unflappable, and he continued to breathe deeply. His face was red and soaked with sweat, and he was thinking hard.

"Cline?" she repeated, louder than before.

He finally snapped out of this trance and calmly looked up and ran his thick hands through his disheveled hair. He looked like someone who had just went through a major battle and came out victorious but still scarred. I guess he had.

"Okay, it's over. Let's all head back to bed," he said like nothing had ever happened.

"I've got to clean up this mess! The kitchen is a wreck, and Lord knows what else there is," Mother said.

"It can wait till tomorrow," he sternly replied. "Besides, they're gone," he added as if he knew for a fact the harm had subsided.

"Oh, Lord! You rile up the kids like that, and now you expect them to sleep?" Mom shot back. "Look at this mess! Look at the kids. They're upset. I am too!"

It was as if Mom was blaming Dad for the whole event. Maybe she thought he had somehow invited them to our doorstep either directly or indirectly. It certainly didn't look that way back then to me.

The way I saw it was simple. He had protected us from some sort of spiritual enemy in my mind, and there was no reason for her to be blaming him for anything.

As we huddled together in the kitchen after everything died down, one look at us and Dad's whole demeanor changed. All that rough and toughness melted away, and a new man was standing before us.

He slowly stood and turned to us.

"It's okay," he said, stooping down to look at the girls. He gently brushed their hair with his big hand and wiped away their tears. "You're safe now. They're gone. You have nothing to fear."

After briefly calming us down, we were all sent back to bed, but, as it turned out, the nightmare had only just begun.

CHAPTER 10
Proof of the Paranormal

Although Dad had said it was nothing, I knew better. I think we all did. As I left the kitchen to head down the hall, I turned back briefly and saw him standing near the patio door staring out into the darkness. He was genuinely concerned himself, so it was hard for me not to be a little worried, as well.

Paul could tell the incident bothered us, so he decided to sleep with Matt and I in our room. One good thing about the location of my room was that I could sometimes catch some of the conversations coming from Mom and Dad's room—when they were alone. Because, believe me, they would watch what they said around us kids.

Their door was almost closed, and the light peaked through the crack between the door and frame.

Clearly, my father had his ideas as to what he thought happened—and my mother had hers.

"Why would they come here, Celeste?"

"I don't know, Cline."

"Those things were pretty low level, but they don't show up for no good reason! There has to be a reason, or they wouldn't have come here like that."

"Well, maybe it's that shit you do or how you teach the kids. Have you ever stopped and thought that just maybe you're inviting this shit into our home, Cline?"

"Enough of that!" he shouted.

Apparently, they realized they were getting too loud because their voices started to trail off.

So many thoughts flooded my mind. Intruders? He was talking about these visitors like they were some sort of spiritual army that had taken up root outside our door.

"You've got this situation all wrong as usual. It's not anything like that," he said, trying to calm her down, but she was having none of it.

A moment of silence passed, then Dad added, "This just doesn't make any sense, unless, that is, there's something you're not telling me, Celeste!"

"Are you really going to turn this around on me?"

"Well, you're obviously not telling me the whole truth. There's something going on, and I'd love to know what that something is, Celeste."

"What do you even mean by that? There's something going on? That makes no sense. You're always trying to turn things around on me."

"I'll tell you one thing, Celeste," he added. The mere fact he kept using her name told me that he was getting more and more pissed while looking for some way to make sense out of what had happened.

"There are boys coming by to see the girls all the time," he added. "Their chores aren't being done when I'm not around. You let them get away with murder."

"That's ridiculous."

"Is it?"

"I think you know the answer to that."

I reflected on what they were arguing about. Much of what he said was true. During the week, Dad was gone, and lately, there were boys coming over to see the girls to allegedly study with them in their rooms. But we all wondered how much studying was actually occurring. It's like he was trying to say that our home—for one reason or the other—had been opened up to spiritual forces, but he also seemed unwilling to recognize what or if he had any role in any of that.

While it's true that sometimes the girls would not even come home after school, Mom would call around trying to find out where they were at. She was at least giving the impression that she was maintaining some sense of control.

At the same time, I didn't realize Dad knew about any of that. As far as Paul, he was now spending all night with his friends. As far as Mom, she always had more things to do away from us kids and was finding new reasons all the time. It's like she wanted any excuse she could find to not be at home or around us. I don' know if that's true, but it certainly felt that way. In fact, it started to cause enough of an issue that Mary eventually complained she was taking care of us more than Mom was.

"What am I supposed to do, Cline? Lock the girls away and throw away that key? That your bright idea?"

"Yea, but you don't even try," he quipped.

That's when the voices came back but stronger and more emphatic than before.

"They have friends. Friends from school. And I am busy. I'm doing more things at the church. The kids are older," she said. "I don't have to be around all the time. I have a life too."

"Oh, that's just lovely, dear," Dad said sarcastically. " Just abandon your duties entirely."

By now, Paul raised his head from his pillow and realized the conversation.

"Hey," he whispered. "It's time to sleep." He immediately jumped from the bed and crept to their door to close it the rest of the way.

"Goodnight!" he sarcastically said, returning to the bed.

I still remember thinking that with Dad's last words, he had opened an entire pandora's box of issues that were going on at the house while he was gone through the week, and Mom went on the defensive.

Up until then, I wasn't even aware that Dad knew what was happening when he was out of town working.

It's hard to describe, but it's almost like he had the place wiretapped. I mean, I'm pretty sure he didn't, but he had the uncanny ability to sense what was happening whether he was physically present or not.

Now, please understand, I'm not picking sides (then or now). I love both my parents dearly, whether I agree with them on certain things or not.

. . .

NONE OF US got much sleep that night. For that reason, we were allowed to sleep in that morning. When I did wake up, Mom was tidying up around the house, and the older kids were doing some cleaning of their own in their bedrooms.

Dad was already outside, and he had a shovel and wheelbarrow full of bags and other miscellaneous items. He would spend the whole day digging holes around the yard.

During the process of filling holes, he chattered the whole time, and once his little concoction was in place and the ground was covered, he would move to the next spot. I wanted so badly to help him, but he would not allow us kids to do anything like that. Plus, he had given Mom strict instructions that we were to stay inside that whole next day.

When he came inside later, he took each one us kids individually and did a chant and burned some kind of root and leaves I'd never seen before.

The smoke billowed up all around us. After doing this with us individually, he did the exact same thing throughout the house.

Mom complained off and on about the smell of the smoke, but Dad was thoroughly committed to the task and continued undeterred as if he was on a mission.

Mom was tough on Dad about his beliefs; however, she also knew that when Dad had his mind made up about a certain thing, that was that. There was no use fighting with him about it.

The whole rest of the day went off pretty much without a hitch. The things they talked about—the fissure they had opened up—was not going to go away anytime soon, though.

Up until the previous night, I still doubted my father's abilities to some degree. I mean, even when it came to the parlor tricks or the weird tricks he did with the dancing flames, somehow in my mind, I would justify what I saw. There had to be some rational explanation for what he was doing.

Well, I guess that's not entirely true.

I did have plenty of questions as to what it all meant, but there's no way in hell that I could doubt my father's abilities any longer. I had seen with my own eyes the fact there was much more to this world than what we "normally" get to see on the physical plane. My appetite for the paranormal had been sparked. I had a hunger for it that—ever since—I cannot fully satiate.

Of course, Dad realized it, even encouraged it to some degree. In many ways, we were like two peas in a pod.

At the same time, I had questions like anyone would, and I didn't know what it all meant. I was so confused. But one thing was for sure, Dad had certainly not lost his abilities. He wasn't doing them around us anymore because he wasn't allowed to. But they were there just beneath the surface.

He was forced to bury this part of his life, which must have been quite tough on him. For him, spirituality and the paranormal were very big parts of his life—and he didn't get to share those things with the people he loved (his children). This is a fact I would eventually know all too well in my own life.

Dad was a man who devoted a good deal of his life to the paranormal in one shape, form, or fashion. It was even his career so far as we could tell. But he had to push all that stuff down and hide it, and I have no doubt that bothered him for a long time. Eventually I was able to have that conversation with him much later in life.

Mom denied the paranormal her entire life (or chose not to accept it). And I never understood that. If you really delve deep into Christian ideas, there's a lot of information about angels, demons, and the divine, as they call it. It's what she and her religion taught us. So, how could you deny it proof of its existence? I mean, just in that one instance, we had more proof with our own eyes than most people will ever see or understand.

Nevertheless, Mom was not going to have anything to do with the paranormal. That much was for sure.

Whatever Dad did seemed to have worked. Or, he was able to keep the bad spiritual forces at bay for a while longer yet. There was never another incident like that again. In fact, the house seemed to have been cleared of anything like the paranormal. As a matter of fact, I never saw the "Prairie Girl" – as I called her, or her brother at the house again.

And despite Dad's success, it was a hollow victory. It was also at this time that Dad's books disappeared off the shelves entirely. We never saw them again. It must have been a hard blow for Dad to take. Slowly, Mom filled the bare shelves with her own books.

There were quite a few other changes going on in and around our house after that night, too. To be fair, they may have come slowly, and I just didn't realize right away, but to me, at the time, it was an all-of-the-sudden thing. To put it mildly, that night was a watershed moment for our little family.

These changes matriculated into how we acted and interacted with one another. For instance, the girls were having boyfriends over, and there was far less worry about how Dad felt about it. And Paul, was either gone most of the time or sleeping really unusual hours as most teenagers often do.

Paul was about to enter his senior year of high school. Mom had more time to be relaxed with our chores and schedules, plus she had even more time away from the house, which seemed to suit her really well.

When Dad was home, they argued more than ever. When Dad asked why the chores were not kept up, my mother would say she was busy and didn't have time to ensure they were getting done anymore.

Grades were slipping across the board.

Dad no longer talked about the spiritual side of things. His morning breakfasts at the kitchen table stopped happening and became him standing at the back door with a cup of coffee around noon.

In fact, overall, there was far less family time spent together, and that saddened me both then and now.

For me, a key sign things had really changed was Dad's garden. When I was younger, he would work a lot outdoors, including the garden. Not anymore.

The garden, which had always been one of Dad's most prized possessions, was overrun with weeds. Dad often slept in, and when he wasn't sleeping, he would drink. And there was no lap time with Dad anymore either.

He was usually asleep in his chair, and we knew not to wake him. Yeah, things were different. My whole normal had shifted once more.

CHAPTER 11
Those Damn Kids

After the incident with Paul in the kitchen, and the incident at night, I think my mom had reached her breaking point -though it didn't occur to me at the time. I admit, taking on five kids was a lot but this was well beyond a wife raising kids while her husband was away. Now, her actions began to show it and it became obvious she had changed. She made no attempt to hide the changes that were occurring like she did before. The façade was gone – at least, to us kids and inside the house. Mom never lost the façade to others. It just wasn't her. What I never came to know was the true cause. Was it just the marriage? The incidents with my father's abilities? Was it just their difference in beliefs? Or maybe, a combination of it all? Either way it was becoming obvious that mom had changed.

It was summer and the other kids were away playing at friends' houses. I was home alone with Mom playing by myself as I often did during those years. I had no idea where she was or if she was around. Then suddenly she was there, basket in hand, and a strange sensation hit me.

"I am going to Tom's to do laundry!" she nervously stated.

Tom was a retired man. He lived next door. We often would go to his house to use the phone when ours wasn't on.

"Okay, great. Can I go?" I replied.

"No!" she yelled. "I'm going to be gone for a while because I have a lot to get done. Now, I made you a PB&J. It's on the counter. You can have that for your lunch. I'll be back in a little while, and you wait right here. Don't come over."

Her words seemed strange to me, and she was incredibly insistent that I didn't come over. I had a strange feeling that something was happening, but I didn't know what, and I was growing increasingly upset.

She had exited the door when I yelled out to her. I didn't want to be alone.

"Mom! Wait, can I please go with you?"

"No, no. It's going to be boring, honey. I'm just doing some laundry. And, to be honest, Tom really doesn't want you kids over there."

She turned around and headed across the patio.

"Why can't you wash the clothes downstairs?" I asked as the strange sensation intensified.

She stopped in her tracks and paused briefly.

A look of disappointment fell across her face.

She slowly turned around as if completely disgusted by me.

"They don't work! Wait here!"

Now, I knew she was lying. Even at age 9 or 10 I was basically a human lie detector system. But, to be honest, it didn't take anything exceptional to spot that lie. I knew the machines worked just fine.

Regardless, it was clear I wasn't going to be going anywhere anytime soon. And, pretty soon, several hours passed.

I ate my sandwich and played in the quiet of the house. But I was starting to get bored and didn't much like being completely by myself. I took hope in the fact that the older kids would be home from playing soon.

But, before long, the sensation hit.

I looked at the phone a few seconds beforehand, and then the phone started to ring. It was if I knew what was going to happen. The whole situation was very odd to me.

"Hello!" I answered.

"David?" my grandmother asked.

"Hi, Grandma!"

"Hi, honey! Is your Mom there?"

It was Grandma, but something was wrong. She didn't ask how I was, how much fun I was having, or what I was up to. I somehow knew that something was terribly wrong and could envision her sitting at the desk at her home with her hand on her forehead.

"She's over at Tom's doing laundry," I said.

"Are the older kids there?" she asked.

"No, they're all gone. I'm all by myself."

"I need you to go get her, okay?"

"Yes, Grandma!"

"It's very important. I need to speak with your Mom."

"Yes ma'am," I replied, sensing the frustration and fear in her voice.

"Run and get her and have her call me back as soon as possible."

I dropped the phone and took off running before she could say another word.

I didn't even grab my shoes. I ran so fast across the field to Tom's house that I think I could have set the word record for the 100 meters.

It seemed like a few seconds later that I was on his porch standing there in my bare feet panting.

I knocked on the door, but there was no answer. So, I knocked some more and waited.

Tom's washer and dryer were on his enclosed back porch. I could see them through his door. There was no basket, and they weren't running.

I knocked again. Again, nothing.

I started to leave, but Grandma had insisted that she talk to Mom, so I knew I had to get her somehow.

We lived very deep in the country, and our neighbors always left the doors unlocked. As a general rule among neighbors in our area, if you knocked and no one answered, you went inside and announced yourself.

Believe it or not, that was considered normal back then.

At that point, if still no one answered or was at home, you would leave a note on their counter or kitchen table. I know. It seems strange now, but that's how things went back then.

So, not thinking anything further about it, I pushed open the door, walked past the quiet washer, and head into the kitchen, looking for Mom or Tom.

"Mom?" I shouted.

Still nothing.

"Mom?" I shouted again.

Not a peep.

I thought maybe they had left, but Tom's car was in the driveway. They had to be inside the house somewhere.

I grabbed a pad and paper in the kitchen and started scribbling a few words.

"Tom, please have Mom call," I wrote.

All of the sudden, I heard a sound.

It was a giggle. No, it was a laugh.

So, someone was home, and I could hear them giggling and laughing and cutting up. They had no clue I was inside the house.

I don't know what they were doing, but it sounded like fun.

I started looking around and trying to follow the voices, and that feeling I had earlier that was subtle skyrocketed inside of me.

I was on the verge of a full-blown panic.

I got near what I believed was Tom's room and stopped and listened. There was another voice. They were in the house after all. So, I made my way to closer to his door and leaned in toward the door. I couldn't quite make out what they were saying, so I finally screamed.

"Mom!" I yelled through the door.

"Shhhh," Tom said.

"Oh shit! It's David," she said.

I grabbed the knob and pulled it open, not knowing any better. That was a big mistake. What I saw haunted me for years. This scene doesn't' really need any further details. I'm sure that you can use your imagination and fill in the blanks.

When I think about it, well, let's just say that I'm haunted. In fact, it took years of therapy for me to be able to open up a little bit and be able to even discuss this topic at all.

I still recall Tom yelling out.

"Well, son of a bitch!" he screamed, jumping from the bed. He ran over to the door and slammed it in my face.

"Go away before I whip your ass! Do you want that?" he yelled through the door as I backed away in shock.

"I have to go, Tom," she said.

"No, no ,you don't! Go away, David, or you're going to get into trouble. Do you want a whipping?"

I don't know what else he said because I had already turned around for the exit. I didn't want to be there any longer than I needed to.

But as I ran away, it's like my legs crumpled and stopped working. I fell to the ground and landed squarely on my face.

I was crying my eyes out when Mom finally came along and scooped me up and threw me over her shoulder and carried me to the door.

"I told you to stay at the house!"

I could not respond. I was so upset.

"You need to go back home!" she shouted again and finally sat me down. "Go!" she yelled, shoving me outside. She then slammed the door behind me.

I gathered myself and made the long journey back across the field to an empty house. I was still upset. Mom had never acted like that. It took me a long time to calm down.

What was that? What if Grandma calls again? I wondered. I was told to get Mom and didn't want grandma mad at me either.

Sometime later, I saw her at the sliding glass door. Unlike before, she was fully clothed, and she didn't have any laundry in her hands this time.

I got upset again when I first saw her through the door, and for some reason, her first words to me were as follows, "I got hot! Tom does not have air conditioning, and I couldn't take it any longer. I almost passed out, so he was trying to help me out."

Look, I knew it was a lie. I was young, but I knew exactly what I saw, and it didn't have anything to do with air conditioning or passing out.

I wanted to scream, "Liar!" But I bit my tongue.

It's no use anyway, I thought.

A dark feeling rose up inside me and totally consumed me.

I was quickly losing interest for "lying adults," especially the ones who were so close to home.

"Go to your room, David. You are in big trouble for what you did. Now go!" her lips flapped, but the feeling was much darker.

Had that thing returned to her? Was it waiting at bay underneath all along? Or was this the change I saw in her?

All these questions ran through my young mind.

She was lying to us now, and the fact that she was not the same before that event in the kitchen was obvious. She had changed. Could she ever be the same again? I didn't think so.

As I walked away, she added a new twist of advice.

"Oh, and if you mention this to your father you need to know the county will come and take you away. You will become an orphan, David. They will take you away from your brothers and sisters and your mom and dad. You will not see us again. EVER! Do you understand?"

I didn't answer her.

For an instant, the creature from the kitchen incident with Paul flashed into my head. I ran down the hall in fear from her and what she was saying. At the time, I couldn't tell if that was another lie or not.

That one threatening phrase would become her go to line for anything she didn't want Dad to know. I wasn't alone. She used it on all of us kids (the fear of being an orphan). It was enough apparently to keep us all in line, too. I never told Dad, although I did suspect he already knew.

And, I never got a chance to tell her that Grandma called. She found out later when she called back again. I don't recall what the call was actually about, but it had to be something important, and I often recall the look Grandma had on her face when she was talking to me. I could see her visibly upset and worried about something. I don't know if she suspected Mom of something or something else entirely, but that's the chain of events that led me to discovering how much my mother had changed.

It was also the time I realized my mother was gone to me. In my mind, she had gone to become a lying adult. So, every single time she spoke, I was reminded of that dark sensation I had that day or when she wielded the hammer like an evil monster in the kitchen. It's hard to shake images like that, and, needless to say, the trust gets completely eroded.

The care I believe she once had for all of us left, and it became so common for her to refer to us as "those damn kids." All us siblings would even joke that "those damn kids" were our middle names. We still do today.

Something was clearly missing from my parent's marriage. I know their marriage was never perfect, and neither of them were perfect people. But, for me, at that time, it was as if Mom had been replaced by someone else, someone who gave me a strange sensation that's hard to describe. Or, maybe, she just finally reached her limit with everything. Afterall, our normal was by no means easy to deal with.

I actually don't aim to cast judgment upon either one of my parents. I can only imagine what sent them on their separate paths and made them react to life the way they did. I agree that life at that time with five kids and a spouse who was gone during the week was stressful, lonely, and cloistered for my mother (not to mention the paranormal factors which must have complicated things). Marriage is hard enough without all of those extra circumstances to deal with.

It would be decades before I fully understood and fully accepted everything that happened back then. But the healing took decades.

Back then, it was just hurt, hate, confusion, and a series of misunderstandings. At the same time, knowing things in advance became my "new normal." It was me, and with time I started to slowly accept who I was becoming, although I struggled to talk about it until much, much later.

CHAPTER 12
The Light Was Still There

My mother continued the charade of what can best be described as a "good Christian woman." My father, at this point, continued down his own path, as well. And he was rarely, if ever, seen.

When he was home, he would sleep in, get up just to drink or go to the bathroom, often falling asleep in his chair in the living room. They never talked or sat at the kitchen table together anymore for their morning breakfasts. Chores were almost non-existent.

On the bright side, if you can call it that, the arguing stopped. I don't think they cared enough about each other to argue. That would have taken some level of caring and it just wasn't there any longer.

Eventually, things got darker, too. Dad was coming home less frequently, and when we questioned Mom about it, she always called him things like "evil," "the devil," or "devil worshipper."

She would talk about him like that, not just to us kids, but also with people at her local church.

Mother would try to normalize things the only way she must have known how. No matter what else was happening, no matter how bad things had gotten, she would try to keep us very active in church.

I later came to understand that was for her benefit more than ours. As a member of the church, you serve your time by knocking door-to-door to "spread the truth of God."

Yes, I was one of those people.

On one such day, we had just emerged from another church service and had headed out to serve. My mother, my siblings, and I prepared to knock on some doors, which was common for us to do. The only thing is that day something strange happened that caught me completely off guard.

We were in service, Mom seemed anxious the whole time. The hymns were playing, and we were singing, but for some reason, she was fidgeting uncontrollably.

After service, in an unusual move, she split us up before going out to serve. That's something that never happened, but this time the older kids went one way, and I went another way. Mother took off with one of the church elders by themselves, and a strange sensation came over me in full force.

I was only about nine- or ten-years-old at the time, and it threw me off. Mom never would leave us alone like that, so I didn't understand what was going on.

So, the day went on, and after service, I finally asked why she did that.

"David, it was not my choice. It was what the elders wanted. And," she said, pausing. "It was what God wanted. And we always do God's will."

A dark tingle swelled up inside, and I knew what she was saying wasn't right.

Although her mouth spoke the words, her thoughts said something entirely different to me. This time I saw flashes of Mom in a car in a bra and underwear with this church elder. Or, maybe it was just the fact that I had caught her with Tom and suspected the worst in her nowadays. But I was shocked and confused, to say the least.

"Come on baby, let's go home!" she said and smiled back at me as she fixed her hair with her hand.

My life was only about one thing during those months, taking care of myself and my younger brother, Matt. Meals weren't fixed, clothes weren't done. We were told if we were hungry, we knew where the food was. Keep in mind, that worked pretty well for the older kids, but it was more of a challenge for the younger ones. Luckily, the older kids would help when they could, especially Mary.

Months would pass before Dad came home again. When he arrived, there was no yelling, no arguments, but it wasn't the Dad I knew. I'm not sure what happened to make him come back home.

Then, my parents decided to throw a gathering with a young couple who was newly married. They were new to the area and living with Tom our neighbor. It was like old times again.

The adults sat at the table drinking and talking as the kids mingled until we were told to leave the room so they could enjoy themselves. As usual, we would sneak back in occasionally to see what was going on. After all, Dad was home, and we wanted to see him.

"That's bullshit!" Steve said. "I want to see it!"

There was some strange excitement brewing, but I didn't know what was going on.

My father, in his deep, gruff voice, quietly and calmly replied, "Maybe later."

So, the night went on. My parents and their new friends were getting pretty loud. It surprised me. It had been a while since Mom and Dad seemed so happy. There was a lot of energy in the house again. I felt like it was a good thing.

Dad finally stood up and looked at Mom.

"Give me the book!" he said.

Steve got noticeably excited.

"You're going to do it?"

He looked at his wife Donna and said, "He's going to do it!"

He was acting like a kid at a candy store.

My mother handed him a phone book off of the stack of extras that we kept, and Dad grabbed it by the binding and rather easily tore it completely in two just like he used to do years ago.

The excitement that erupted around the table was priceless.

"That's not all!" Mother added with a smile.

"There's more?" Steve questioned.

"Show them the light!" Mother proudly added.

"Let's go outside!" he said, grinning, something he rarely did anymore.

In a frenzy, the room cleared, and us kids quietly tagged along. Moments later, we were all standing on the back patio, kids included.

It was a rare occasion that us kids were included in what was going on with the adults, so I was beyond thrilled.

"What are you going to do, Dad?" I asked.

Dad bent over. I expected to be told to go back inside.

"Watch the dusk-to-dawn light," he said with a grin. Then, he pressed his finger to his lips, telling me to be quiet.

My sensation began to ring. The electric fell over my skin and then moved all throughout my body. What was about to happen?

My father turned to the light and began to focus. I stood there watching the glow from the light on this big post. Was he going to hit it with a rock? He had a good aim. What was he going to do? I wondered.

I could barely contain myself.

"Quiet down," Dad said gruffly, calming the excitement.

He concentrated on the dusk-to-dawn light that ran down the sidewalk from our driveway to our patio. His focus was brief but intense. In silence, I watched as the light bulb went off. It was great! It was amazing! I want to do that! I thought.

And the whole crowd erupted. Incredible! I thought.

The light started flickering and seemed to want to come back on. I could feel the energy in the air moving all around me and vibrating through me and off of my skin.

"Wooo!" Donna yelled. "That's amazing."

"Wait! Wait! Wait!" Steven said, cutting the excitement. "How do I know you don't have it on a switch or something? One of the kids is in the garage or something turning it off?"

The heightened energy in the air began to subside.

The crowd silenced.

Dad had this stare. It was one of those stares you really didn't want to see from the opposite end. It was either because you had doubted him, he thought you lied, or he thought you were a total dumb ass.

He gave Steven the stare, and, I was glad it was him getting the treatment and not me.

"What?" Dad bluntly replied. "The kids are all here. Everyone is right here," he added, pointing.

Steven took count of the people on the patio with his eyes.

"It could be a defective sensor on top making it go off or something!" he proclaimed matter-of-factly.

An argument ensured.

It started to get heated. Father shared his gift with you, I thought, and you doubt him? I was not liking this Steven guy one bit, and I wasn't alone in that line of thinking.

I felt the whole energy start to turn.

"Hold on!" Dad said, grinning like a cat ready to pounce. "You tell me when to do it then?"

"What?" Steven replied.

"You," Dad said, putting his large finger into the chest of Steven's thin body. "You tell me when to do it, and I'll do it."

There it is. The energy settled back down.

"Okay," Steven replied, all prepared to prove Dad was a fraud.

Mother had a grin from ear to ear at this point. She was proud of Dad. I had not seen her smile like that for a long time, especially as it concerned Dad or anything Dad did.

The energy and excitement started to build all over again.

Dad hushed us once again.

"Now! Now! Now! Now!" Steven said, gunshot style.

Dad looked at him in disbelief.

"You have to wait for the light to reset between times!" Father informed him.

"Oh."

Dad turned to us kids as if Steven was some sucker that didn't know any better.

"Kids, watch the light bulb itself. Pay attention."

And with that the energy began to build again, and we anxiously clung to his every word.

We stood there waiting, staring at the light. It seemed like minutes passed.

Then out of the silence, Steven yelled, "Now!"

Boom, the light went off. But this time, I noticed the bulb itself was black. Yet there was still light as if the bulb was on.

We stood in hurried anticipation, watching the light slowly reset. Steven started a conversation with his wife then as if to throw Dad off, but he stopped mid-sentence and yelled, "Now!"

Again, the light went off. The bulb was completely dark, but the light was still there.

Steven would test Dad repeatedly for what seemed like an hour, and each time, the light went out. In the end, Steven was grinning from ear to ear. He was no longer doubting my father.

"You're amazing!" Steven said, trying to slap Dad in the middle of his back.

My father just grinned back. Then, shortly afterward, he said something to the neighbor. Dad and Mom turned to us kids, and the energy changed again.

"You kids take the little ones inside. We are going over to Tom's. See that you go to bed by 10:30!"

And just like that, the adults were heading across the field to Tom's house.

We went inside and played games and laughed. Paul showed us some magic tricks he had been practicing. At some point, I snuck away and went outside. Tom's house was lit up from one end to the other. Even his bedroom light was on. The music was loud, and his windows were wide open.

I actually wasn't mad they left the house and went over there. To be honest, it gave me a warm, peaceful feeling seeing Mom and Dad having fun together again.

. . .

THE NEXT MORNING was a whole different story. I woke up early and made my way into the kitchen. The energy was thick and had a dark, ominous tone.

I almost hesitated to go all the way into the kitchen. Mom and Dad were sitting at the table like they used to do, which was nice. But then everything changed. They stopped talking as soon as I entered the room. In fact, they didn't even acknowledge me.

There was a dark energy and silence between the two of them the rest of the day. It was like they had a grudge match going on between the two of them that was lurking just beneath the surface but barely bubbling over.

The sensation I felt never escalated but never subsided either. In addition, I noticed Dad was back to his high ball cocktails once again. And it was with the family sitting around the dinner table that Mom made an announcement.

"Your father slept with Donna Fuse!" she regurgitated into the silence.

We all stopped in shock.

"Celeste!" Dad yelled.

"Well, it's true. You couldn't keep your hands off that young girl, could you?"

Silence was my father's way of letting you know he was angry. It was his punishment to you. He was a man of very few words anyway. His stature usually did all of his talking. Silence was a tool he would often use to get what he wanted or prove a point (that and his stare). My father sat there in silence, while Mom began spouting on and on about his alleged indiscretions with Donna.

"Come on, let's go," Mary said, grabbing my hand. We all went off to our rooms to play while they continued to argue.

At that point, Dad seemed like the bad guy. He certainly wasn't perfect. It wasn't until decades later that the siblings and I compared notes and came to the belief that our parents were actually swingers. Apparently, within that realm, there are certain rules and permissions, as well as certain things that were totally off-limits.

For Mom, Donna Fuse must have been one of those limits. Or maybe it was just simple, old fashioned jealousy.

Either way, Dad did something that Mom was openly struggling to deal with despite her own infidelities.

CHAPTER 13
Circling the Drain

I think I must have tossed and turned for at least an hour before my body and mind eventually gave way. However, at one point, I woke up to a loud noise and sat up quickly. At first, I felt like it must just be the trees whipping in the breeze, but then that familiar sensation came back.

In this dream-like state, I was in a cold place that was blacker than a moonless, overcast night. I was feeling my way forward as if I'd been stricken blind.

Where was I? I wondered.

I was completely lost. Then my eyes adjusted, and I realized I was in my bedroom, but it was much darker than normal. No window. I could hear distant conversation, almost whispers that were beyond my reach lost amidst the darkness.

I hopped from my bed and worked my way slowly through the darkness and out into the hall.

In my constant anxiety, I was hoping for treasure, peace, tranquility. I was tired of the torment and just wanted a sweet peace, the kind that only comes from being completely comfortable with one's self and surroundings.

However, an uneasiness started to settle back in, and I could now see my own breaths in the cold air.

I knew I had to get out, so I continued to fumble through the nearly impenetrable darkness, feeling with my hands that were extended out in front of my face, moving this way and that. As I slowly moved forward, a subtle red glow pierced the darkness at the end of the hall.

Arms outstretched, I felt my way toward the light. The whole living room was now aglow with this red light as if it was guiding me. I could hear the piano playing in the distance, and I crept my way closer. There sat Dad with his back to me attempting to play.

I looked around. My mother and several other people were gathered around the piano as Dad performed. I walked my way toward the crowd as they laughed with their backs to me.

He must have sensed I was there because he turned to me with dark eyes and said. "Are you ready to learn?"

I was horrified! The crowd began to laugh, and it was then I noticed they all had black eyes, and they were all piercing down at me. I wanted to shrink down so small they couldn't see me.

The hairs on my arms stood at attention, and I finally bolted from the living room as Dad continued to pound random notes at the piano.

The crowd got louder with laughter as I struggled to get away, but the hall seemed unusually long this night.

The more I ran, the farther I got from my bedroom door, and I kept running and crying, trying to get away from the torment that their laughter represented.

I finally stopped in my tracks, ready to completely give myself up to whatever they wanted.

Now the kitchen was also ablaze with the same red glow. And I darted past the table and then froze at the patio door. I stared out the door and into the blackness of the backyard and woods as the laughter from the living room slowly dissipated.

I noticed a glow that was far away in the distance, gently lighting the woods with an evil-red light. It got brighter and brighter until silhouettes of people in robes began to appear. They were marching around in perfect unison.

There must have been hundreds of them because the whole woods were glowing red from their torches. I watched in fear as they marched their way down the trail out of the woods, making their way toward our house.

They were mounting another attack.

Three of the glowing silhouettes stepped forward shoulder-to-shoulder and approached the patio door. No faces could be seen. I stood petrified as these faceless beings approached. My throat started to tighten, and I gasped for breaths. Instinctively, I clenched at my throat as the air completely escaped me.

My heart was pounding.

It seemed like minutes before they moved, and then I started seeing them gather around the first three. Quickly, the middle one stepped forward and then thrust itself at the door.

I stumbled and fell backward but somehow managed to catch my fall. When I looked up, it's face was pressed hard against the glass. Its eyes were glowing red, and its demonic face was twisted and distorted.

I had to escape.

I stumbled to my feet and then shot down the hall. This time I made it back to my room with the horrific echoing of laughter chasing me.

I instinctively ran to my bed, and plunged into the sheets, but instead of landing in the warmth of my bed, I was immersed in an icy pond.

My breaths had completely escaped me, and I stared up at the ice that was at the surface, as well as the faint, familiar red glow from the demon's torches in the background.

Oh my God, I'm drowning.

I beat on the ice with my hands, but it would not break. Then there were silhouettes moving above me on the ice. Was it Paul again coming to save me? Then, between my hands, a face was pressed. The same dark demonic face with Red glowing eyes from the backyard. I was so terrorized, I pushed away from the ice. And then I realized, there appeared to be hundreds of them pressed against the ice.

This is it. I'm going to die. Paul's not here to save me this time, I thought.

I could feel the life pouring out of me as the water moved around my body.

No! Not again!

I started to slowly sink further and further down until my feet finally hit the bottom of the pond.

There was one last glimmer of hope. I finally decided I was going to confront those evil things and take them down with me, so I started flailing my arms, trying to fight my way back to the surface.

When I finally reached the surface I reached for the ice and grabbed ahold, but it quickly broke free in my hand, and I started to sink again.

I felt the last bit of air in my lungs. If I was in a dream, I wanted someone to wake me from this horrible hell before it was too late.

I stared up at the ice again with the distant haze of the red torches glowing in the distance. The water was so cold that my shaking finally ceased, and I felt completely frozen in terror.

One. Last. Scream, I thought and plunged back toward the surface in one last effort to emerge.

I roared and screamed as my head emerged from the icy pond.

All of the sudden, the faint, red glow of the torches had been replaced with a bright, white light that was burning my eye lids.

I was lying in bed dripping wet with sweat and panting.

I was no longer drowning, and as the air hit my lungs, I knew I was alive and well.

A familiar voice called out to me, but I didn't know who it was. I tried to look up, but the light was still too bright, and I couldn't get them to adjust.

I understood in that instant that I no longer had to seek anything anymore. Everything I was searching for was staring right back at me and the warm of the night air hit my skin and comforted me to my core.

In some weird way, I knew that I was standing defiantly in the presence of my own enlightenment. This kingdom of joy and peace was mine for the taking if I was willing to accept it.

All I had to do was let in the light and allow it to wash over me and comfort me and warm me.

"Come to my voice," it said.

That's when I tried to move, but I realized there was a chain attached to my ankle. I set up in bed and started tugging at it, as the voice continued to call out.

The frustration was starting to mount. I mean, I was right there. It was within reach. I was alive and well, but I was stuck to my bed so tightly that I could barely wiggle around.

This was a prison of my own devising.

"Wake up!" the voice cried out.

"Wake up!"

I pulled at the chain once more and then fell to the ground. When I looked around, there was a dark hole in the floor, and the water was swirling around it like a drain.

I tried to stumble to my feet, but I was slowly slipping away and getting closer and closer toward the drain.

The pressure was starting to mount. It was like a crushing weight that was pushing against me, choking the life right out of me.

"Wake up!" the voice repeated.

I now understood what it was saying, but I was trapped in some darkness, tethered to death, like an anchor pulling at my feet, sucking me into the drain.

I tried to scream, but I couldn't make out the words.

"Wake up!" the voice screamed louder than before. "Wake up, David. You're having a nightmare."

I looked up and realized it was my mother staring back at me.

Oh my God, I am free, I thought.

"You're so sweaty, David. What's going on?"

My body was drenched in sweat like I had been swimming with all of my clothes on. Maybe I had been. In hindsight, that must have been a dream, but it felt so real.

I could feel the life being squeezed out of me as I swirled around the drain.

I often struggled coming to grips with my mother, who she was, what all she had done. But maybe she really did want the best for us. The only thing was, what was best for us differed greatly between her and Dad. He had a whole different version of what best for us looked like.

That night, my mother's voice led me out of the darkness and toward the light. I've sometimes resented her, but one thing is clear: she did love me, and she spent the rest of the night making sure I was alright. I cannot tell you how good that made me feel.

CHAPTER 14

Hello, Dad

Dad left later that weekend, and it seemed like a really long time before he returned. And, when he did, it was obvious that something was going on.

For one, their marriage was clearly broken and beyond repair. I didn't realize it until I was much older, but it was in that stage where both parties know it is over but are afraid to call it done. The relationship between them seemed to just be lingering in that state. But there was something additional to what he and Mom were dealing with.

Could it be something spiritual? I often wondered. He was a very spiritual man, but he wasn't showing any signs of his spirituality anymore.

That steady calmness he always seemed to possess was non-existent. He seemed on the verge of blowing up at any time. He was struggling, but with what I didn't know.

He was also drinking a lot more. My parents seldom talked to one another. Everything was different. Even Dad began to spiral out of control. He closed himself off from the family, something that was not like him at all. He spent his weekends drinking alone and his nights awake while the rest of us slept.

One afternoon, in the middle of a drinking binge, he caught me coming through the kitchen. Mom was working hard nearby at dinner.

"David! Come here," he said in a drunken stupor while tapping his hands on his lap. At 11, I felt a little too old to be sitting on the old man's lap, and I didn't like him when he drank. It smelled really bad—and it impaired his speech. It just wasn't the him he truly was and had always been!

But he was still my father, so I dared not to disobey him. I hopped on his lap. In front of him was a glass of high ball, his preferred drink, and it was almost empty.

"I'm going to show you how to make my drink for me. You're old enough to learn," he muttered. He began to show me what portions of alcohol to soda to use. "Voila! There ya go!" he exclaimed. "Now, next time I call you, I want you to make it that exact same way. You hear me?"

"Okay," I shyly replied, really not wanting to have to remember how to make it.

"Cline, you shouldn't show him those kinds of things!" Mom said, bringing the cutting board of scraps to the trash near the table in front of us. She started scraping them off with the knife.

Dad looked down at me and winked. As quickly as he winked the ashtray sitting on the table before us slid across the table and shattered against the wall next to my mother. She jumped back horrified.

He began laughing a huge, raucous laughter.

"Cline! Did you throw that?" she angrily asked.

"I didn't touch it!" he replied, looking back at me and grinning. *True, he didn't. He really didn't touch*, I thought.

I didn't like him like this. It wasn't him. Mother walked back to the other side of the room to the stove. After briefly checking things, she shouted.

"Nathan!" she exclaimed. "Did you turn off my burners?"

Dad only replied with a giggle.

"Why the hell would you do that? Here I am trying to cook dinner, and you are playing your games."

I was getting increasingly uncomfortable by the minute.

Please stop, Dad. Please stop, I thought.

He just sat there calmly drinking his high ball. I slowly slid off his lap and went into the living room to play.

A short time later, he entered the room. He stopped in front of the windows and started staring outside.

"Cel! Who the hell is parked in the driveway?"

"It's one of the kids Paul goes to school with," she replied from the kitchen.

"Well, who the hell is he?"

"He's from the neighborhood."

"Why is he here?"

Mother mumbled something below her breath, then she got louder.

"Football! He's here playing football with the other kids."

Paul often had his friends from school over to play football, and our field was the perfect makeshift playing field.

I would sometimes beg to play myself only to be dragged down the field or kicked in the face while holding on for dear life to someone's ankles. It was all I could do at a young age not to die while out there on the field with those much bigger kids who were seniors in high school by that time.

Dad calmly walked out of the living room and apparently snuck up to Mom from behind and scared the hell out of her. I could hear them laughing about it a few seconds later. I felt relieved that the tension had subsided.

As I went through the kitchen to go out the back door they were standing at the stove, arms around one another occasionally sharing kisses.

Although I didn't know it at the time, it would be the last time I saw the two of them acting lovingly toward one another.

Later that night after, the older kids left, and Mom, Dad, Matt, and I sat in the basement near the old fireplace. The pops and crackles of the fire reminded me of times when things were different. As I sat on the fireplace ledge to the side, I looked around the room and watched Mom and Dad in their lawn chairs watching the fire together. The light flicked on their faces almost romantically. It was almost like old times. I thought briefly that there was a chance that things could return like they used to be. But it never lasted.

It was just the fleeting hopes of a small child.

Mom and Dad were talking about the rest of the weekend and Dad returning to work.

Then, Mom said one sentence that changed everything. She lovingly looked at my father and said, "And I am so glad all of your bullshit is behind us."

You could feel the mood change in one fell swoop.

The look on my father's face will forever be burned into my memory.

"Excuse me? What bullshit?"

Oh, no.

My mother stammered for a minute to capture the right words, but my father would have none of it.

"Come on Cel? What Bullshit?"

Again, Mom stammered.

"I meant that all our problems," she gulped loudly. "That the problems are behind us."

"Oh," Dad replied, but I felt like he wasn't buying it.

Just as things appeared to be settling down, my mother began to regurgitate and spew a string of sentences as if they were poison coming from her mortal soul.

"I mean, we have put your hokey religious beliefs behind us! Now, you just need to start attending church. And I can introduce you to—"

She stopped talking. I guess she sensed the same frustration growing inside Dad that I could.

She had been rambling so quick it was not as if he could get a word in to disagree anyway.

Was it the fact she called his beliefs hokey? Was it something else? I wondered.

Well, I never found out. Dad just sat there. I could literally see him boiling, and it was at the same moment I noticed the fire grow brighter.

"Oh, and then we can get you baptized again," she added.

Just as the words left her mouth, a ball of fire shot out from the fireplace, knocking her backward.

Matt and I were stunned.

My father, who had been seated beside her, had gotten up and walked upstairs. Before we could get Mom off the floor, we heard him close the garage door and leave.

No words. No arguing. He had left in a blaze of glory (pardon the cliché). But that's what happened.

I guess he couldn't take it anymore. Did he intentionally cause the fireball to rise up and blast Mom or did his temper get the best of him?

There was a series of events that soon followed. For one, Paul graduated from school and went off to join the Navy. Both my sisters got pregnant and married. And my parents finally got separated.

I think the little talk in the basement that day was the final straw for the two of them. It would prove impossible for Dad to have his family when his family was gone with their own. And their beliefs were just too far apart to bridge.

When he finally left, I missed him dearly, and it's not easy talking about it even today.

Worst of all, our whole home environment changed after the older ones left. I don't know if it was a mass exodus because Dad had also left, or if things just happened that way. In either case, our house was empty, and it seemed to happen slowly and then all at once.

I was younger than the older kids. They were off and away. Just gone as if a magician did a trick and POOF they disappeared. At age 11 you do not have a choice but to be stuck. And I was stuck. Stuck with the situation, stuck at the house, stuck without dad to talk to and guide me, stuck with no decision in the choices made, and stuck at home with mom and Matt.

The house seemed quieter and more depressing than ever. The house that was once abuzz with activity all the time was now silent, still, almost – dare I say it – haunted by the activity of the past. I know at least I was. And I think each one of us was haunted by the situation and past memories of what once was and could be no more. I believe we all kind of mourned for those past times. And as usual, there was no discussion. We all did it independently, in silence.

This was our new normal, I had no choice but to just accept it. But just as I was beginning to come to grips with things, Dad had a couple of "party tricks" left that he needed to do, as well.

. . .

IT WAS A warm summer night. The windows were open as they often were during the summer. Dad and the older kids had been gone for quite some time, and it was just the three of us left behind.

Mother had taken to having a couple of friends from church come over. One of them was allegedly fixing something, but the only thing I caught him fixing was his pants as he staggered down the hallway.

He briefly said hello and left. Apparently, he was a little bit embarrassed. Turns out, he was one of the married ones.

So much had changed in my life, and we had no real answers as to what was occurring. *Where was Dad? What was going on? Who were these new friends that Mom had?* I wondered.

One night, we were sitting in the kitchen, and I got the impression that Mom was willing to talk, so I jumped at the opportunity.

"When is Dad coming home?"

"I don't know, David."

"Why not?"

"I don't know. I don't know that he will ever come back," she admitted.

"Why?"

"I don't know," she said, lying.

"Well, who are these guys?"

By the look that came across her face, I could tell she was not amused by my question, nor did she want to answer it.

"David!" she bluntly replied.

What? Did I say something wrong? I wondered.

I was about age 11 by then, and it's just not an age that you fully understand certain things. I was naive to the situation and a lot of things because of my upbringing.

But I figured that maybe she'd do better talking about Dad. She didn't seem so upset about that.

"Does Dad know your friends?" I asked innocently.

She was starting to get agitated, and finally, she got up from the table and started to pace.

"David, I don't know."

"Why did he leave?" I asked, feeling a tear form in the corner of my eye.

"David, please stop!"

"I want to see Dad!"

She paced quicker.

"Why are you doing this now?"

"I just want to see him. Are you mad at him?"

That was her breaking point.

"Your father is a bad man! I don't know how else to say this, but he's an evil man!" she yelled. "He's a Devil Worshiper. He is pure evil!"

A strange sensation fell all over me again.

She was claiming that my father was a "devil worshipper." That was something that she'd say anytime she was mad at him, but I don't know if she believed it or not.

She went on to explain to me that, in her opinion, his abilities came from him doing evil things. She said he got his gifts from "worshipping evil," and to back up her belief, she began to tell me a story I had only heard bits and pieces of before.

She told me that before I was born, they lived in a small town in Illinois. She woke up one night to find him fully awake and talking to a demon at the end of their bed. She said once she woke and saw it, she gasped, and it disappeared. Father was apparently angry that she chased it away. She then said that she demanded him to get rid of all his "devil-worshipping books" the very next day and stop all his "devil-worshipping activities."

She stated that when Dad refused to do so, she grabbed them from the shelves herself and threw them in a burn barrel, threw gasoline all over them, and dropped a match on them.

She explained that, for some reason, the match didn't catch the books on fire at first even though she used nearly a whole gallon of gas on them. She tried again. Time and again there was no fire. Then, she said, the wind finally kicked up and a great storm blew through, and, in typical fashion of every good horror film ever, she said her final attempts to burn them were extinguished.

Frustrated, she went back inside to find the books were back on the shelves. In fact, they were perfectly dry, she said, as if they had never left their original spot.

I'm telling you right here and now, I did not believe her.

But she asked me if I ever noticed his books all had burned edges. I thought long and hard about what she said. I knew the books she was talking about.

They were the same ones on the family bookshelf I'd looked at some many times before (until she got rid of them). The corners of several of those old books were darkened and looked burnt. I used to ask Dad about them, and one day he showed them to me up close. Many of them were scorched and had burnt ends from where she had tried to set them on fire.

Later, my older siblings would confirm this story also. I do believe Mom's story now.

But, more importantly, that old bookcase was like our family and represented the divisions that existed between my parents and their belief systems.

Finally, his books went away.

Finally, he went away, as well.

Where his books once stood now stood other books, one's Mom approved and placed there.

Was that what she was doing with her new friends? Finding ones she approved of more than dad?

The whole story she had either concocted or relayed to me was absolute confirmation of his evilness in her mind.

But, to me, even then, it made absolutely no sense at all. He still did his parties tricks with us kids. And I saw the pride in her eyes in his abilities. I saw the smiles on her face when he did them because she knew he was one of the only people in the world who could do what he did.

So, how could she feel it was evil or devil worshipping from the very beginning? Was she deeply unsure about her own faith? I wondered.

She added that there were things even us kids didn't know about Dad and Dad's abilities. She explained that his abilities went well beyond simple "party tricks," but it was better we just left it at that.

She even admitted there were probably things she had no knowledge of him being able to achieve herself and that she feared him and what he was capable of.

That part of the story I believe. She did fear him, not so much that he was ever violent, because I never saw much in the way of physical violence in our house. But she did fear his spirituality, his beliefs, and his abilities.

"Those were not cheap parlor games or tricks," she said.

Then suddenly she was in a frenzy like I had never seen her.

She was practically foaming at the mouth as she spouted out things about him. But there was something I had never seen with her before, especially when talking about my father or his abilities.

"Please listen to me," she cautioned. She swallowed deeply. She was scared. "I questioned whether to tell you this, but he's watching this house and listening to our conversations. Look, do you see that faceprint on the window?" she said, pointing to the garage door window.

I looked over to see the imprint of a nose, eyes, and chin on the glass. "That's him! He was watching us right there!"

At first, I thought she meant he had the place watched or bugged. I came to realize differently.

"He is watching me like a hawk! The son of a bitch is probably watching us right this second! I hope you're listening! Do you hear me you son of a bitch!" she yelled, looking all over the house like a madman.

There was silence for a brief second.

Then the kitchen sink turned on in full force.

It was Dad.

It was him confirming subtly that he was there.

She let out a scream that sounded like someone getting murdered. It pierced my ears, and I cupped them shut with my hands.

I closed my eyes and continued to cover my ears, hoping she'd stop screaming and calm down.

"Leave us alone you son of a bitch!" she yelled, looking around.

Finally, there was something in the air again. The room was reenergized, and a calmness fell over me.

Mother collapsed to the floor in an emotional mess while I walked over to the sink.

As I turned off the water, I smiled and said, "Hello, Dad!" It may sound strange, but without a doubt I knew it was him. I knew his abilities.

I walked back into the kitchen, watching her on the floor. I shook my head and turned and walked away.

That one event changed her more than anything else ever could. Her world was totally different. He had really gotten into her head. Even though he was physically gone—he was still there with us in spirit, and there was no denying it. It shook her to her spiritual core I believe to this day.

I don't think she really understood or fully comprehended what all my father was capable of until that moment. I mean, clearly, she had her suspicions, but that faucet didn't turn itself on.

For us kids, we just accepted things like that as our "normal."

It was.

It was Dad, and even when he wasn't present, he was present. He was almost omniscient and omnipresent.

Mom believed deeply in God and in religion. That's how things worked and should be. But that event finally helped her to throw all that out the window and quit ignoring there was something unusual going on and always had been.

As you read this, I'm sure that many of you will have several "WTF" moments. For me, for us, for my siblings, this was our normal as I've noted. It was as normal for us as if I told you that people can walk and talk.

For us, in that house, at that time, it's just how things were. We knew that he had unusual skills and that sometimes people would revel in those acts. We just didn't get the full weight of it until later.

It was not until years or decades later that the skills my father had and the unusual aspects his life would come to be fully understood (including the work he performed).

CHAPTER 15
My Saving Grace

As you have no doubt noticed, this is a book about the paranormal and how it surrounded me throughout my life. However, there were other events that impacted me, as well, and I grappled with whether or not to include them. I ultimately decided that leaving some of them out would not allow me to paint a full picture of who I am as a person, or the full impact these events had on my life. For that reason, it was important for me to include some of these events.

So, things were rapidly changing on the home front. The older kids were gone. My parents had divorced. Mom seemed to be hanging onto her sanity by a thread. Not only that, our family was permanently banned from the church because of the divorce, which must have been incredibly hard on my mother. Up until then, she lived for the church, but divorce was a deal breaker for them. It was forbidden without exception. Her own religion, her own spiritual compass- the one that she jumped through hoops to work for her (and us) – abandoned her when she needed them the most.

Our house was also about to go into foreclosure. Looming in the near future, we knew we were going to have to move away from the family home as well as the only hometown I ever really knew.

Changes were swift and drastic, but no portrait of my life would be complete without including the following.

After a string of childlike and obviously over-sexualized relationships, Mom finally met a young man who was ten years her junior.

Allen seemed genuinely interested in her and us, but I could tell there was more there with him than met the eye. He was nothing like my father, and he was an alcoholic, which concerned me greatly.

I never got a dark sense around him, but I cannot say I got a great feeling about him either. Apparently, the feelings were mutual. As an alcoholic he took his issues out on everyone around him. And as the oldest kid in the home at that point, I typically got the brunt end of his attention.

I was big enough to halfway stick up for myself. I cannot tell you the numerous times Allen would seemingly befriend me for a specific task such as helping him grab something in town or to help do some kind of work. But it was only to drop me at the store to shop while he headed off to the local bar.

One day, he came back in a drunk-driving stooper and picked a fight with me. He actually beat me about senseless and then dumped me on the shoulder of the road to deal with the situation for myself.

When I got home, Mom told me his story. He had told her that while he was shopping, I went missing, and he had to leave without me after putting on a valiant search (I guess the injuries were made up too).

No matter what was said, Mom always went along with the stories she was fed from him.

My father was completely out of my life by then. I was stuck with the drunken asshole and a mother that was more of a partner in his crimes than anything else. She was acting like nothing more than an immature teenager.

There were wild parties every weekend and drunken strangers flopping out in our home. And, apparently, she thought it was a good idea to fully explore her sexuality versus finish raising her children.

Some of the parties could have put the wildest frat house parties to shame, and I had even started drinking openly myself. It was a glutenous feeding frenzy, including mountains of drugs, alcohol, and sex.

Mom was hardly ever around. And when she was, her attention was not with Matt and me. At least, not as a parent.

A few regular party goers who knew my family before all this would come around and make sure that there was some food in the house to pick through. Beyond that, we were quite literally on our own. Matt and I took care of each other to the best of our limited abilities.

Sometimes there was no electric. But there would be kegs of beer lying around as well as various other beer and alcohol, BBQ, and places for people to crash. My brother and I even had to give up our room and beds for the cause.

It was during that time that one of the male party goers took an interest in me. At first, it started with him slipping me some beers, then he would justify me drinking to my mother. Believe me, the justification needed was very minimal.

Then, like wolves on the hunt, other people got interested, too, or word got out. Some of the more sensitive details are long and dark and not for this book. But I will say this: the abuse was really bad for many years. Even when it was reported to my mother, I was told, "We all do things we don't like in life."

So, I never brought it up to her again.

She brushed it off as either a lie or me making something large out of something small. In reality, it was probably too much of a threat to what she wanted at that time, so she chose to keep the party going versus deal with it.

My gift left me as the abuse and alcohol entered the picture. I came to learn those things do not mix well. I was in a very dark place as a kid. The thought of suicide entered my life. It felt like I had been fed to the wolves.

I was used to perpetuate the situation my mother was involved in at the time no matter how wrong, dark, or twisted things became. I was basically an offering to keep things going. Things got so mixed up that I figured if my own mother didn't want me, I should at least be glad someone did.

The only reason I include these things is because some good did come from it. It's hard to believe, I know, but ultimately it would shape me into a more positive direction.

I credit a few things with really saving my life through the years. First, Paul, swooped in and pulled me from the icy waters.

Around the age of thirteen, I moved in with my grandparents, which I credit with saving my life (more on this to come).

Counseling has also helped me along the way.

The last thing that I credit with saving my life was *her*. She was my saving grace. Now, I will not mention *her* by name, but I will say that most people have no clue how bad things had become. They have no clue how dark things got and how close I came to ending it all on numerous occasions.

Those of us who have glimpsed pure evil recognize it easily. Those of us who have survived something really bad like that also recognize other people who have experienced it, too.

Survivors of abuse share a common bond, a set of experiences that are not quite the same thing but very similar. For those on the outside looking in, the mere discussion of these things may reframe their thinking and demonstrate how ugly the world can be. For others, it is inconceivable, if not altogether impossible to grasp.

For anyone who's quick to pass judgement, I hope you left on page two or before, because I am sure that your critical thoughts of me will not subside as we proceed into the following pages.

In fact, I am sure they will be fed further. The following events may repulse you. Certainly, they can be considered (or are) criminal, or borderline-criminal, at the least. But again, life is about all those little intimate experiences that we endure, and I didn't think my story would be complete without them. Moreover, writing this book and sharing my story has been therapeutic for me, and I only hope that it will help others, too, who may understand precisely what I'm talking about.

I've had some counseling, and it's only now that I can openly talk about what happened. For some people, everything is really clear and black and white. But sometimes all those conventional lines of right and wrong get muddied and grey.

I know the darkness I was in. I know the circumstances that dragged me into the darkest depths and held me there until I was completely devoid of any prospect for a life that was worth living.

But I also know the relief and the values that come afterward.

My life would drastically change because of these events, and I am the person before you today because of what occurred. So, for those reasons alone, I have no reason to hide.

. . .

ABUSE BECAME normal to me. As strange as it sounds to type these words, I know it's true. I had come to accept it. One of my regular abusers even started bringing his girlfriend to the parties.

I was fine with it because it meant I got less of his attention. She was a very beautiful, sweet girl who came from the country. She had a kind, slow, southern drawl. She treated me well and everyone else she encountered. In fact, she became like family to us over time.

One night Mom went out with Allen. The abuser (whose real name isn't important to this story) and his girlfriend had been called to watch Matt and me. So, we headed out with them to eat. As she got up to walk Matt to the bathroom, a plan was sprung on me.

"She is going to, um, well, you know," he said, stammering.

I was shocked and thought it was a joke. Was he serious? I nervously giggled back at him.

"No, I'm serious! You're going to be moving soon, and you are older. You need to know some things, and she is going to show you. Trust me, you'll be glad she did."

Again, I laughed. I looked at her waiting outside the bathroom door for Matt. She acted no differently.

Did she know? Was he lying?

"Okay! Don't believe me, but you'll see!"

I was so nervous I could no longer eat. The table was quiet the rest of the time with only him looking up and smiling at me occasionally as if he knew some terrible secret.

After dinner, it was a long, slow ride back to the house.

I remained quiet.

As we got closer to the house, she turned around in her seat and looked at me.

"So, what do you think?" she said.

Did she know what was sprung on me? Was she in on it? I wondered.

When she saw I was not responding she turned around. Pretty soon, we got home, and briefly, I thought it was all behind me. It wasn't going to happen. The joke was on me, and everyone was in on it but me.

Matt had fallen asleep on the way back, and once we got there, she took him to bed.

We then settled in on the couch and watched TV. The next thing I knew, he re-entered the room fully naked.

"Are you ready for this?"

I was shocked and covered my eyes.

"Hey, it's okay," he said trying to pull my hands away. When he saw that he was not getting me to budge, he relied on her.

"Talk to him," he said. "Make him feel more comfortable."

With her accent and soft voice, she coaxed my hand down.

"It's okay! It's fine," she said, leaning into my ear. "It's perfectly normal!"

There was that word again, *normal*.

"Aren't you even curious about girls? Boobs?" he said.

"Yes," I replied.

"Do you want to see her boobs?"

I began to shy away and hide my eyes.

"Quit!" she said to him. "Let me talk to him."

He moved away and sat in a chair nearby.

"Hey," she said, pulling my hands down.

"Do you think I'm pretty?" she asked.

I was at that awkward in between age. Sex had been in my life since I was six, and I always had an interest in women as long as I recall. When she entered our lives, I would often take advantage of getting a hug from her just to smell her or feel her press against me. The whole way I looked at her and other women was changing, and I didn't know why.

Pretty? Yeah, I think you are beautiful, I thought to myself.

However, my reply was a soft, "Yep!"

"Do you want to kiss me?" she asked, seductively.

I started to shy away again.

"Hey! You've seen things. You know what happens here. You know girls and guys get naked together! Come on!" he said jumping up from the chair.

She quickly shushed him.

"Hey, why don't you go away for a little bit while we get more comfortable?" she asked, and, to my surprise, he reluctantly left.

She looked back at me though my fingers which were loosely covering my eyes. I looked back into her eyes.

"Come on, kiss me!" she said, taunting me by pressing her lips together. "It's okay! Don't you want to?"

"You won't tell Mom?"

She laughed slightly.

"Nobody's gonna know but us."

I finally caved and took my hand off my eyes and leaned into her for a kiss. As I drew away, I could tell she was holding back a laugh through her smile. Hey, it was my first kiss unless you count my grandmother or mother.

"That was good," she said, lying. "But now I want you to try to do something a little bit different. Let me show you."

She coached me how to hold my lips, what to do with my hands, my tongue, everything. No stone was left unturned as we navigated the subtle nuances of how to kiss and pet.

To be honest, her soft pouty lips excited me, and once we began, I didn't want to stop kissing her.

This is fun, I thought.

Things slowly progressed from there, and she slowly began to undress herself and then me. As we made out, he returned to the room and pulled out the couch and threw some covers on top. Before things could get really started there was a knock at the back door. He was fighting to step back into his pants as we he went to grab it.

I was lying anxiously next to her, naked. I was waiting to see what was next, waiting to see if we were caught, waiting to see what trouble was coming our way.

My heart was pounding so hard in my chest I was convinced she could hear it—and was going to laugh at me for being so nervous.

The person at the door turned out to be an old family friend he knew from school. It was a small town, so everyone knew everyone.

They quickly got involved in a conversation.

When it was obvious he wasn't going to return anytime soon, she started back in.

She taught me how to be tender with a girl and kiss her body, how to use my hands, and so much more. I was entranced in the moment and didn't want it to end.

I remember thinking it was as if the world was finally making sense to me. This is why adults are so silly and get all wrapped up in each other.

Needless to say, it was unlike anything I ever experienced.

First, this was not *normal* to me. She was a female. Suddenly there were these thick, pouty, subtle lips, kissing me all over. Then the curves, which were in all the right directions. She was a tender, delicate creature, plus she was kind and considerate and responded to my touch.

She would explain and ask questions. She seemed to genuinely care about how I felt and was concerned about what I wanted. It was a give and take kind of thing, not the one-sided, incomplete, unfeeling experience I was used to.

And while it was different than anything I had ever felt, it also seemed like exactly what I needed in my life at that moment.

He was having a long in-depth conversation in the other room apparently. Fortunately, or unfortunately, she was not quiet and made a little too much noise. Her recovery was excellent though, and she quickly hopped from the bed and threw her shirt on.

"Throw the covers over your head in case he comes in here," she whispered, giving me a quick kiss on the cheek. And she quickly darted into the other room to cover up what was happening.

"I just had to finish without you," she said as she left me behind and entered the other room.

There were some giggles, and I can only imagine what he thought or what the family friend thought. I actually giggled, too.

I ended up laying there in total amazement. My head was spinning about what happened. This was the thing I was looking for, the thing I needed in my life, and it changed everything in an instant.

It seemed like an eternity before the guest left. They both entered back into the living room and approached the fold out couch where I was waiting.

"So, now we can get started," he anxiously said, pulling back off his pants and hoping into bed.

"Actually, I'm kind of tired now," she quipped.

"What?"

"I'm kind of tired! You spent over an hour talking! I'm tired now, and I just want to go to sleep."

I saw the disappointment fall across his face. I was waiting for an argument, but it never came. She just took off her shirt and hopped between the two of us naked.

He clicked off the light and a short time later she angrily said from the darkness, "I said I was tired."

I laid there in absolute bliss, feeling her bare skin gently press up against mine. I didn't know if it was really love or just sex or something else entirely. But I knew it was something I wanted repeatedly and for the rest of my life. I felt happy, safe, and full of bliss.

In the light of day things were back to normal. No one mentioned or acted like anything happened. I was used to that but had questions. *Did she regret it?* I wondered. *Was she denying it?*

Mom returned late in the morning after everyone was awake and dressed. Soon, he and she were gone.

Before she left, she gave me the normal hug goodbye and then very gently kissed me on the cheek and paused.

"See you later, sweetie," she whispered, and then she left.

. . .

IN THE HOURS and days that passed, all my thoughts were about *her. When would I see her again? What would it be like? Can we do that all over again?* I wondered.

The next weekend finally arrived and both he and she offered to watch me again, so that Allen and Mom could go out. Mom never passed up a chance to leave us kids, so she jumped at the opportunity.

"Yes!" she snapped, not even contemplating the where. She was just happy to get away again.

This whole thing between me, her, and him became a regular routine for about six weeks.

The two of them would look for any reason they could find to separate me from my mother or volunteer to babysit. I noticed how she would often interject herself between me and him before things could start between us.

Did she know about him? About us and what was really happening? I feared.

He didn't seem very happy about it. Of course, I didn't mind. I wanted her regardless. He was just the thing I had to put up with to get to her.

The routine started to settle in when he showed up one day and announced that he had broken up with her.

I was crushed.

In my nervousness, I figured I would never get to see her again!

Of course, he very quickly moved on to someone new. However, his attempts to bring a new her into the picture was a total fail. I denied, dodged, excused my way out of it every single time. I didn't want a substitute for *her.*

I wanted her!

In my mind, my time dealing with him was over. But she was gone too! It was a harsh price to pay to remove him from my life.

And then one day out of the blue there was a different car in the driveway. Seconds later, she was standing at my door. In the excitement of the moment, I wanted to rush to her and throw my arms around her neck. I never wanted to let her go again! I knew I could though. I had to wait and see what was happening.

I didn't know what to expect. She quickly made her way in after a brief knock. Mom welcomed her with a hug, and they were off in conversation. I just sat nearby and watched and listened. I noticed her eyes occasionally catch mine without Mom seeing.

Ah, she was back. Back in our lives, I reveled.

"Well, I just wanted to come by and take you guys out for ice cream and show you my new car," she said.

"Oh honey! I can't leave now. Allen's going to be home soon," Mom said. She went on to explain something, but her exact words were lost on me. All I was hearing were excuses so that I couldn't spend time with her.

"Well, shoot," she replied. "Well, I guess you can come look at my car at least?"

She was very crafty and quick witted. And we headed outside toward the car.

We stood there admiring it for several minutes and not saying too much. When things were winding down, she said, "It'd be great if I could at least take the boys out for ice cream."

She knew Matt was not around. She didn't see him. *What was she doing?* I wondered. I felt another *no* coming from Mom, but she knew what she was doing.

"Matt's not here, so sorry babe. It will have to wait for another day."

My hopes sank as the words left Mom's mouth filling the warm, muggy air.

"Well, honestly, I was hoping to get help moving a dresser at my apartment. I was thinking David could help me. I would bring him right back?"

"Can I Mom?"

There was no fear of being caught, no fear of what was going to happen, only the bliss that she was here, in front of me, and asking me to go with her.

"Sure," Mom relented. "Go help her and come right back! Your step-father is going to be home soon, so don't be gone too long."

And just like that we were off. I wasted no time and jumped into the passenger side seat. She climbed into the driver's seat and shot me a quick glance and grinned.

Smart thinking! I thought. She was a crafty one.

The ride in the car was fairly quiet with only a cursory word or two here and there. Honestly, I didn't really know what to say or do. I was probably scared if I said anything it'd be the wrong thing, too.

I wasn't sure if she was thinking what I was thinking or if she really had a dresser to move. So, I just rode along content that we were together again—and he was nowhere around.

CHAPTER 16
An Alternate Ending

In the days that followed I was in heaven. I would sneak off to her place under the pretense I was meeting with friends, or going to town, or having some ice cream. I found out really fast just how quick witted I could be when it came to finding excuses to see her. She would come up with a range of excuses herself like helping paint her apartment or needing help finding someone. It didn't matter as long as it meant we would spend time together.

Her tenderness, consideration, and conversation were just what I needed. It was really the first time in my life that I shared any sort of close, intimate experiences with a member of the opposite sex.

It's like having a veil pulled back from your eyes as you realize everything life has to offer for the very first time. Though I was still drinking and dealing with certain negative aspects of the past, I was beginning to feel normal again.

For a spell, the paranormal had actually left my life, and I was happier without it. All I cared about was spending time with *her*.

I never had that before. People would talk at me, order me around, or demand I do things. She talked to me, not at me, if that makes sense. We connected in ways that were unlike anything I'd ever experienced before.

Most people would come to me with tasks or tell me what to do. She would come to me with concerns, issues, or genuine discussions. When I would talk, I noticed that she would stare back at me and actually take interest in what I had to say. To this day, I still cherish good conversation as one of the sweet gifts in life, and I credit that to *her*.

Now, there was a difference in our age, but not that much really. He liked his girls young – I can only assume for obvious reasons, so she was only a couple of years older than me. At a different age, it would have been totally acceptable. And by no means did my current age fully represent my maturity level given all that I'd been through.

At the same time, I can understand why some readers may listen to my story and think about what happened to me like I was being used, or manipulated, or abused, or some of all three. They may even call her a pedophile.

I can't change how you feel about HER no matter what I say. And you can call it what you will, but the fact is she saved my life. Only I know the darkness I was in and living with. I had no future ahead of me at that point. I had almost given up. I was on the brink of suicide.

Had she not entered my life at that exact time I can honestly say that I would not be breathing right now. I would not be right here with you communicating my story to you today. She quite literally gave my life an alternate ending than the one I would have had.

This story would have ended a long time ago (probably somewhere around chapters three or four I would have been another sexually abused child who succumbed to the pain and took his own life.

I would be data on a sheet somewhere and easily forgotten about. *How sad would that be?*

You may be wondering, what's the difference between what he (or the others) did and what she did? In a word: outcomes. Let me explain.

I walk, talk, and breath air because of her. I am a better person because of the tenderness, love, and compassion she showed me. No one else was showing me that! She came in at just the right time and showed me that the world had so much more to offer, something much greater than darkness and pain.

She approached me with kindness and consideration, something the others never did. With him- and the others, I never had any choices. My innocence was taken, and there was no regard for the cost those actions had on me. So, I was a thing to them.

They came along, got what they wanted, and quickly discarded me. They did not better me in any way whatsoever. To me, that's a big difference between what *they* did and what *she* did.

Those are two vastly different accounts.

Because of *her*, I have a profound respect for women. I wasn't going to respect women (at least back then), not given my circumstances, not given my mother. My mother showed me no reason to respect a woman. She displayed that we, as people, take from other people. There's zero thought for what they might need or accountability for the actions or outcomes. So, there was no way I would be able to adequately understand, much less have any respect, for women up until that point in my life.

Think about it. My sisters were gone and out of my life. All the other female family members lived very far away and were rarely heard from. From other girls—like at the parties my mother used to throw—I was shown they were just something for guys to take advantage of for what they wanted. They had no intrinsic value to me at that point because they had no intrinsic value to other people. And the women who were in my life were either non-existent or not worthy of respect. Especially with my lack of trust with anyone I considered an "adult".

Don't get me wrong. I'm not saying any of that is okay. It certainly isn't. The point is I had no good female influences in my life until she came through my door. It would have been hard for me to come into a truer, more accurate understanding of what women need and want aside from being something physical that's used up and discarded until the next one comes along.

For the record, my father had provided a decent example to begin with as far as adult men were concerned. But it was minimal as he was always gone. And it had been quite some time since he was in my life anyway.

For me, at that point, females were not something to be respected, and she changed that, and that's why what *she* did and what *they* did were two very different things in my opinion. As noted, it comes down to outcomes.

Every time I got to see her the rush was incredible. There were no cell phones or internet back then. If there had been, I doubt we could have afforded them anyway. But there would be these unplanned, surprise meetings we didn't know were going to happen that were pleasant and blissful when they happened—and always highly anticipated.

It was pure bliss, but, unfortunately, it didn't last long. The time we spent together would only represent a small sliver of my overall story—but that's not to diminish her role as a lead character in that story.

To this day, it is still kind of hard to accept the loss of her and the way it came about. It was so unexpected. I don't know if it was the same for her or not.

The day she left, I had hurried into town to go to her apartment. I ran up to the door and started knocking at the door like a madman.

I guess I was so excited to see her that I failed to notice her car was missing from outside. As I knocked a few more times the door finally pushed opened. It wasn't locked. So, I ended up standing there peering inside from the doorway. There was no movement, and I quickly called out to her.

Still no movement.

I waited for a minute or so and then finally let myself all the way in and slowly walked around the apartment. Not only was she not there, her stuff was not there either. Everything was in disarray. There were a few empty paint cans and supplies left in the sink. It looked like she had left—and hurriedly.

Whatever had happened, it was pretty clear. She was gone. And the weight of her leaving hit me so hard that I nearly collapsed to the floor and started sobbing.

Was she was truly gone? Would she return? I wondered. *What happened to her? Why was she not here?*

To be clear, I never got an answer to my questions (at least not from her). Time delivered the answers cruelly.

The whole way home (and afterward) I cried and cried until I almost ran out of tears. All manner of thoughts ran through my mind. We had talked about her fears, our situation, what it meant to her, what it meant to me, and how other people would see things. Everything was going so well between us—and then BAM! She was gone.

Naturally, I started to blame myself, which is what I always did.

Did she leave because of me? Did she think I was going to leave her? Or tell? Was the situation too much for her?

. . .

FOR A LONG TIME I held out hope that she would return to me. But days quickly turned into weeks which turned into months. And she never returned.

I mourned for her much like someone mourns the death of a loved one.

The whole experience of losing her was unlike anything I'd ever gone through in my life. There was a range of emotions from pain to sadness to agonizing grief. However, I can say this. During this time, the thought of suicide never once returned, which is a testament to how much she had changed my life to the positive in my short time with her.

It's not easy to say, but I think a lot of it was just knowing she was out there somewhere that hurt so bad. Did she really choose not to be with me? Did her fear get her? Her departure felt like a death to me, but at the same time, I knew she was alive and likely well, so I found some small amount of solace in that fact alone.

I was also able to find joy in what she taught me about life. She opened up the world to me and showed me what living felt like. She removed all the darkness that had brought me to a very bad place in my life; and, in her own special way, she removed part of the stench of *him* and the pain he caused me.

Chapter 17
The Summer of Normal

Amidst the process of grieving for her, my mother sprung on us that we were going to stay the summer with our grandparents. At the time, I cannot say I was looking forward to leaving our home at all, but it did make a good cover for why I was so upset.

By this time, I was a teenager. The world had just opened up to me in a lot of good ways. And to leave friends and my hometown for the summer was not something that appealed to me at all.

Don't get me wrong. I knew eventually we would have to move, but I was hoping to spend one last summer with my friends in the town I had known my entire life.

My grandparents and other relatives were kind loving people. They were all strict Catholics. They were upstanding people in their communities. Grandfather worked for the steel company. He started out as a temporary worker, moved his way up, and eventually retired from that same company with a modest pension.

Aside from my parents, my family put the "model" into "model citizens." And they had always lived so far enough away that our exposure to them was limited.

So, we didn't know what to expect when we arrived. Visits to them were precarious and short lived. There was an understanding that we were not to talk about Dad's "party tricks," the wild parties, or anything else that occurred behind the closed doors of our home that would make most sane people cringe.

The rule was simple: if we didn't talk about it at school or to other people, we didn't talk about it to our grandparents or other relatives.

I would also sometimes wonder how my mother fell so far from the family tree. It was amazing. Maybe things were just too perfect or too strict for her. In any case, the idea of the city for the summer and watching what we had to say and do was completely unappealing to me. And I was sure there was going to be rules. There was always rules when it came to adults.

I'm sure for my mother it was even worse. She could fool us kids (or thought she could) but fooling other adults with her phony charade was something else entirely, and there was no way she was going to pull it off.

When we did arrive, it was more of a drop off at high speed. (Should we have expected anything less?) It was five minutes of "Hi. Here's their bags. Be good. Bye for now!"

The one thing I could look forward to was that we had friends from the church in the neighborhood, the Meijer's. Before my family moved away, my mother and Mrs. Meijer became good friends. Her sons were around our age, so we became friends, too, including Greg who was my age.

He and I had practically grown up together because every visit to our grandparents was a chance to play and see each other. So, I knew I wasn't starting from total scratch with friends, which helped.

Although it was rough and odd at first, Greg and I would become even closer. We spent the summer riding bikes all over the city. He introduced me to more people, and eventually, we had a solid group of friends. We started cutting grass together to make money so we could do more things. We went roller skating, bowling, and played tennis and racquetball for hours. There was so much to do in the city, and it was starting to grow on me.

Greg's family even had a pool. And eventually, he talked me into getting back in the water. As long as I could touch bottom, I wasn't afraid.

By the end of summer, with his patience, I learned how to swim, something I had been afraid to do my entire life due to the frozen pond. I felt like I was cheating death every time I swam. The fear of water was finally gone and had no control over me.

There was even a girl interested in me, so life was getting pretty good.

My grandfather became the consistent male figure that I never had, considering Dad was almost always working. I didn't have anyone to tell me about cars, watch sports, show me how to throw a ball, or other "masculine" endeavors. I learned how to check and change oil, work on a mower, fix things around the house, and more. There wasn't a week that went by that we weren't going to either the auto parts store or the hardware store.

Grandma showed me how to cook and explained to me that it was okay for a man to do that. She told me Italian men showed the women in their lives how much they loved them by preparing special meals for them. I went shopping with her and she would tell stories of meeting Grandpa and how to be a proper gentleman.

At the store, she would show me how to pick out the best fruits, vegetables, and meats. There are a lot of stories I could share about Grandma and Grandpa, but they're not directly related to my paranormal life, so I chose to keep this section concise.

I will say, staying with my grandparents also pulled me back from the brink. They gave us routine (and not in a bad way). We knew when we came home what we had to do, and we did it. No fuss. We knew we would have electricity and plenty of food to eat. We knew there wasn't going to be strangers at all hours of the night. No parties. No drugs. No alcohol. And no abuse.

Okay, there was still the occasional alcohol. We were Italian and allowed a very small glass of wine with meals. Not to mention the occasional party, but it was nothing like my old life. And when it did occur, it was my choice.

Mother would call out of the blue sometimes. It was never scheduled or expected. As the summer went on, I became too busy to even want to talk to her anymore. With all those Italian Sunday dinners and having a regular routine, my brother and I were practically new people.

We finally had the love and support we'd been missing for so many years. I'm very grateful to my grandparents and all my other relatives for being there for us.

That summer, I began to feel like I was part of a family. I had support and friends. I had people that wanted me in their lives and not for the wrong reasons.

I went that whole summer with nothing paranormal happening. At the time, I found it odd that people really don't talk about paranormal events. It wasn't normal to them. It just showed me how normal and accepting it became for me, along with all the other dark and negative things. That type of normal was a distant memory. And as the summer went on, none of it even crossed my mind.

That summer I felt the most normal I had ever felt in my life up until that point. I realized that I had caught a quick glimpse of what normal must look like for other people.

However, just as quickly as it had started, the summer was drawing to a close. We knew our time with the normal we came to know was about to end. I warned all my friends that it was coming all summer, but once it came it was really depressing.

My brother and I had to say goodbye to our friends, and we packed up our clothes and waited nervously for mother's arrival.

Of course, mother arrived like it was a big event with Allen in tow. She rushed to both of us and gave us kisses and hugs as if she had missed us. Maybe she had. It had been a very long time since she had done anything like that.

Had she changed? Would things be different when we returned? Or was this all a show she was putting on for everyone? I wondered.

The adults spent hours talking and laughing. My mother always had stories to tell and loved telling them. Our grandparents bragged on how good we had done and how we had helped around the house.

After dinner and while the adults talked and cleaned up, I took the opportunity to sneak away and spend time in my bedroom one last time. I thought about leaving my bike behind, one Greg had given me because I didn't have one. He was such a good friend! My thoughts began to turn toward what life would be like returning "home."

What events would happen, sending us back to the dark places we had cleared from our minds? Would we be prepared? Would things be even worse now that we knew what normal was like?

"Hey kiddo!" Mom said as she stood at the doorway.

Kiddo? I wondered.

That was Dad's word, and I had never heard her say it. But I noticed she was almost meek, apologetic even.

I sat up on the bed and she approached. I sensed something was going on.

She sat on the edge of the bed and grabbed my hand as I instinctively cowered down.

I think she noticed my hesitancy and her expression softened.

"How are you doing?" she asked as she rubbed the top of my hand.

The truth was I was upset to leave my friends.

"I'm okay," I said as I started to tear up. I fought it. I didn't know what was going on. And I was not going to give her a chance to see me cry.

"It's okay," she softly replied. "I know you're upset about leaving."

I just shook my head yes.

"You liked spending time with Grandma and Grandpa, didn't you?"

Again, fighting back tears, I quietly shook my head yes.

"Well," she said and paused. "I have something to tell you."

A lump formed in my throat. This was not good. A million thoughts went through my mind.

What is it now? Is she taking us to an orphanage? I wondered.

If that was going to be the case, I would have preferred to stay right there.

My thoughts raced to all kind of horrible places. I had just spent a normal summer with normal people and finally had to leave this normal life that felt pretty damn good to be honest.

There was no sex, no drugs, no strange people in our house at all hours of the night. A nice normal life!

What is she springing on us now? I wondered, looking up from the bed hesitantly.

I knew she was hesitant to say what she needed to. *Just fucking say it*, I thought.

She sensed my mounting frustration starting to spill over.

Shyly, she said, "Oh, it's not anything bad."

But I knew that was a lie. My skin began to tingle, and my sensation began to ring heavily in my ears. Something was definitely wrong. She gave one last pat on the top of my hand before she finally revealed the truth.

"I already sold the house and we are moving up here," she said, pausing. "Right now!"

The words finally fell out of her mouth, and I realized what was wrong. It wasn't the words she used or how she said it. It wasn't even the fact that I was not going to be able to return to the town and friends I left one last time. I wasn't even mad that as the words left her lips she smiled at me as if she was giving me some great present.

There was no time to react to or get angry about what she said. Because as the last words fell from her lips an old friend from home returned. The Prairie girl poked her head out from behind her and grinned.

Chapter 18
One Piece of the Puzzle

Some of you may be wondering, "Hey, what's up with your Dad?" Sure enough, I've often wondered that same thing, too. What did he do for a living? What happened since the events of this story? What about the Prairie Girl? There are so many unfinished questions, and I totally understand.

Please let me explain.

This one book represents a five-year process. I struggled from inside the first year whether or not I should even write it or not. I was comfortable with it, but would others be?

Despite the growth in acceptance with the paranormal field, I had seen changes in the field and not all of them have been good. In fact, to date, I still get warned about how my story could be torn to shreds because of the competitive nature of the field and all the online hate that occurs.

There were countless people who warned me not to write this book. No, not because of the story, but because of the way people are today and how they might take it. In some ways, hate may even be more acceptable now than ever before as people cower behind their keyboards and phony online personas.

Well, that isn't me! However, it is why I intentionally do not post my evidence or share a lot about what I do publicly. So, admittedly, this book stands in stark contradiction to all of that.

At the same time, I have received ample generous support, as well. There are friends who I never expected to support me as I rallied to do this book. The really strange thing is, many of them never knew this side of me until I announced I was doing this project.

As it occurs, I am a very private person and even some of my closest friends had no idea that I dealt with the paranormal or how long I had been into it or why.

175

I've even had family come forward to encourage me to tell my story. Truthfully, why wouldn't anyone accept it? It is a story worth telling.

Regardless, I have spent many years keeping my mouth shut from the sidelines. I watched the paranormal field advance in many good and bad ways and took no part in any of it.

My belief has always been that every person holds a piece of the paranormal puzzle, a piece that could advance the field or give someone else's experiences more meaning. Yet here I was holding my experiences up my sleeve like a poker player, which contradicted my beliefs.

Since deciding to move forward with this project, I struggled with how to tell it, what parts to include, and even how much of each part. The paranormal was a fraction of my life, not my whole life, at least, not at the point I chose to cut off with the final scene at my grandparent's house.

There is so much more that did not make the book, some paranormal, some not. This is where Adam J. Siders came in as my editor and friend. He helped to keep me focused and guide me on the way. For that I say, "Thank You A.J.!"

But that was not my only struggle. During the last nine months, I lost two close friends—and then the pandemic hit. The world was dealing with Covid-19 and the resulting aftermath. Routines had to change. Everyone's life has changed, and the whole project was slightly derailed and almost brought to a dead stop.

In fact, as I write these final words, my family is under a second mandated quarantine for the potential exposure to the virus. OUR normal has now shifted once more.

My intent was to tell my whole story when I started. However, no one would want to buy it because of its length. Honestly, I know I wouldn't. It would require either one really long book or several volumes.

So, that was something I struggled with. I wanted to tell my whole story, and I wanted to put it all in ONE book. And to be honest, I could have done it, but I think the much-needed details and depth of the story would have suffered greatly.

And I was not willing to compromise the story. For me, the depth and details are the story. It was then that, with the assistance of Adam, I came to realize that it would take multiple books to tell the full story. Not the ideal situation, but necessary.

So, I apologize, for ending the book where I did and leaving you with so many questions. There is so much more to tell. The depth and reveal of my father is an interesting one that will come. We honestly had no clue what was going on with him or the details of his work. We came to learn a little bit about it, and I would love to share more sometime.

Another surprise was how my life would come to parallel his.

My mother's journey is not revealed either and it should be. What you might find surprising is she is still in my life. Again, that would be another journey to be revealed.

My siblings also had their own journeys. I cannot tell or talk of their struggles or their unique perspectives even though a lot of those things seem to match my own. I consciously avoided talking too much about them in this book. For me, it is their story to tell. This was about my journey and my perspective on what happened.

Lastly, you must be wondering, what happened to me? I'm really not one of those adults who looks back on his childhood and cries about why their parent's marriage didn't work out or the rough life I had. Look, it happens. We make plans and sometimes those plans don't work out. Afterall, all of our normals are different from each other as well as our expectations.

I also don't beat myself up any longer about some of my experiences (including the assaults). This is isn't something I run from because I am a survivor. In fact, I do talk about those things quite often. I am a sum of all the little bits and pieces of my experiences and relationships, the good, the bad, and the indifferent.

I won't give too many more details because I have to save some of them for the coming book or books. I will say basically what you can find on your own. I do deal with the paranormal practically daily.

I know some of you are thinking that I must be messed up beyond repair. Actually, the opposite is true. I am a trained therapist and energy healer. And, for the record, I never believe someone is beyond repair. As to what got me from point A to point B? Well, again, details are important for context, and therefore, I will tell that tale in the coming book or books. So, please stay tuned. In the meantime, thank you for embarking on this journey with me.

Appendix
Acknowledgements and Special Thanks

First, and surprisingly, I have to thank my parents. I know, it's a shock. They gave me the best love they had to give and did their best to do it right. Though it wasn't perfect, it put me on the path that lead me to where I am today, and today, I know I am exactly where I should be. Thank you!

Next, my siblings! We were all as different as anyone could be and yet we supported one another through it all. We were forged in fire together. Your support is part of the foundation that I stand on to this day. Thanks for your support and love through it all!

To my friends who have rallied forward without knowing things before my announcement, thank you! Your support and love has been amazing!

To my grandparents and my other relatives. Though they are gone from this earth, I still want to acknowledge them today (as I do every day) for delivering the love and support we needed and at just the right time. Your love lives on with us and through us each day!

To the many people throughout my life who have fed my soul, lifted me up, and supported me along the way, thank you. I may not mention you by name, but your impact on my life is realized and appreciated.

And finally, to my loving wife, my kids, and my family. Your support and love has made this all possible. You supported me, even when my normal sometimes scared you. It was only with that unwavering support that I could attempt to do any of this. Your support through the ups and downs kept me motivated to keep striving for more. And your love through everything makes me a better person. I am who I am because of you all. Thank you all for your true and honest love!

Made in the USA
Monee, IL
25 August 2020